An ordinary life
in practice

An ordinary life in practice

Developing comprehensive community-based
services for people with learning disabilities

Edited by
DAVID TOWELL

King Edward's Hospital Fund for London

© 1988 King Edward's Hospital Fund for London

Printed and bound in England by Hollen Street Press

ISBN 1 870551 10 9

King's Fund Publishing Office
14 Palace Court
London W2 4HT

Contents

Notes on contributors   7

Introduction   9

**Part One: Revaluing people with learning
                disabilities**

  1 Exploring values as the basis for service
       development   23
       Paul Williams and Alan Tyne

  2 Involving people with learning
       disabilities   32
       Chris Gathercole

**Part Two: Designing, developing and safeguarding
                high quality services**

  3 A community approach to serving
       children and their families   45
       Philippa Russell

* 4 An ordinary home life   59
       Ritchard Brazil and Nan Carle

⚹ 5 Developing opportunities for an
       ordinary community life   68
       Linda Ward

⚹ 6 Promoting opportunities for employment   80
       Jan Porterfield

  7 What it's like for us   90
       Alice Etherington, Keven Hall and Emma Whelan

  8 Serving people with very challenging
       behaviour   96
       Janet Maher and Oliver Russell

  9 Safeguarding quality   106
       Roger Blunden

Part Three: Achieving large-scale change

 10 Generating policy and action   119
       Chris Gathercole, Tom McLean and David Whalley

11 Training for service development   129
    Jim Mansell

12 Managing strategic change   141
    David Towell

Appendix I   Publications in the 'An ordinary life' series   159

Appendix II Further reading   161

Roger Blunden is Project Leader, Long Term and Community Care at the King's Fund Centre for Health Services Development. He previously directed the Mental Handicap in Wales Applied Research Unit.

Ritchard Brazil is a Fellow at the King's Fund College and runs the College's programme on strategies for developing community-based services for people with learning disabilities.

Nan Carle is a Fellow at the King's Fund College and previously directed services for people with a mental handicap, Lewisham and North Southwark District Health Authority.

Alice Etherington is a member of People First and chairs a Camden self-advocacy group.

Chris Gathercole is Top Grade Clinical Psychologist with Blackburn, Hyndburn and Ribble Valley Health Authority. He chaired the King's Fund working group on 'An ordinary working life'.

Keven Hall is Secretary of the Trainees' Council at the Edgware Social Education Centre and a member of Barnet MENCAP.

Tom McLean is Director of Nursing Services at Calderstones in the Burnley, Pendle and Rossendale Health Authority and chairs the North Western Regional Health Authority Mental Handicap Advisory Group.

Janet Maher is Top Grade Psychologist in the Bristol and Western Health Authority and General Manager of the Mental Handicap Sub-unit.

Jim Mansell has a joint appointment between the University of Kent at Canterbury and South East Thames Regional Health Authority with responsibility for staff training in services for people with learning disabilities.

Jan Porterfield works independently in training and consultancy on services for people with learning disabilities. She is Adviser on Mental Handicap to the Joseph Rowntree Memorial Trust.

Oliver Russell is Consultant Senior Lecturer in Mental Health at the University of Bristol and Honorary Consultant Psychiatrist to the Bristol and Weston Health Authority.

Philippa Russell is Principal Officer, Voluntary Council for Handicapped Children and chairs the Independent Development Council for People with Mental Handicap.

David Towell is Fellow in Health Policy and Development at the King's Fund College and a founder member of the Independent Development Council for People with Mental Handicap.

Alan Tyne is Director of the Community and Mental Handicap Educational and Research Association and was responsible for introducing systematic training on the principles of normalisation to Britain.

Linda Ward is Research Fellow in the Department of Mental Health, University of Bristol and was involved in producing the Open University/MENCAP course for parents and staff, 'Mental handicap: patterns for living'.

David Whalley is Assistant Director of Nursing Services at Calderstones in the Burnley, Pendle and Rossendale Health Authority.

Emma Whelan lives and works in London, likes going out with friends and enjoys travelling. She speaks regularly on her experiences at conferences.

Paul Williams is Associate Director of the Community and Mental Handicap Educational and Research Association. He is co-author (with B Shoultz) of *We Can Speak for Ourselves*, a book on self-advocacy by people with learning disabilities.

Introduction

In February 1980 the King's Fund published *An Ordinary Life*. This was the first element in what has become a continuing series of contributions to ideas on the design of local services for people with learning disabilities. More importantly, this work is part of a broader movement seeking to achieve fundamental improvements in the quality of these services. The paper included a powerful statement setting out the intentions of the group which produced it:

> Our goal is to see mentally handicapped people in the mainstream of life, living in ordinary houses, in ordinary streets, with the same range of choices as any citizen, and mixing as equals with the other, and mostly not handicapped members of their own community.

The title of *An Ordinary Life* represented this goal and has become a way of symbolising the philosophy upon which a genuinely community-based pattern of services could be constructed.

In the ensuing eight years this philosophy has been taken up in a wide range of local initiatives. Aspirations towards 'an ordinary life' are now almost commonplace in the plans of health and local authorities. Some of the innovative services which have resulted are sufficiently well-established to have been the subject of systematic evaluation. Recently, particularly through the re-location of provision based in NHS institutions, the pace of change has been accelerating so that over much of England and Wales large-scale movement towards local services is now under way.

However, after so many years of inappropriate and under-funded provision, the *revaluation* of people with learning disabilities (that is, the proper recognition of their rights as fellow citizens) and widespread development of community-based services are major undertakings. Recent progress, made somewhat against the tide of growing disadvantage for many people in the UK, can only be regarded as the first phase in a much longer programme. While what has been done already on a small scale demonstrates the possibility of principled change, it remains an open question whether the achievements of these innovative services can be sustained, built upon and generalised.

In part, of course, further progress will depend on political commitment and its expression in government policies, not least to ensure adequate funding for high quality provision. Equally important is continuing growth in a range of energetic local initiatives designed to secure real gains for people with learning disabilities and their families. If sufficiently widespread, such initiatives can themselves influence national policies and increase the priority given to these services. Moreover, purposeful local action is essential if available opportunities are to be used to good effect.

An Ordinary Life in Practice has been produced both to encourage and support these local activities. Reflecting on the best of what has been achieved so far in the 1980s, the contributors review key issues raised in the 'an ordinary life' series and examine current practice in providing different components in a comprehensive pattern of community-based services. Recognising that progress depends on action through coalitions which involve a wide range of interests – people with learning disabilities, their advocates and relatives, community representatives, people from voluntary organisations, professional staff, managers and members in the public agencies – the text has been written in a way intended to make the book widely accessible.

AN ORDINARY LIFE – IDEAS INTO ACTION

As with most multi-faceted programmes of social change, the 'an ordinary life' initiative was shaped by a variety of influences and has now widened to embrace an extensive network of people and activities. Viewed from the King's Fund it had its origins in the late 1970s, when Joan Rush, Andrea Whittaker and I (all then working at the King's Fund Centre) became aware of a growing number of enquiries from people seeking precise information about the different ways in which local services for people with learning disabilities might develop. In many places, the paucity of existing services and the shortage of resources were leading to a search for approaches which did not necessarily demand major building work. In others, significant investments were being planned but local people were concerned that this welcome input of resources might largely end up in a new pattern of mini-institutions, whether provided by the NHS, local authorities or the private sector. These concerns were reinforced by a number of national developments pointing to the need for informed innovation. Most explicit was the philosophy and model of care advocated in the *Report of the Committee of Enquiry into Mental Handicap Nursing and Care* (Parliament 1979). The government's subsequent endorsement of this philosophy, its legislation to provide financial mechanisms to speed up the transition towards care in the community and specific commitments, like that to bring the remaining children and young people out of mental handicap hospitals, added further impetus. Also at national level, the articulate voice of CMH (the Campaign for People with Mental Handicaps) and specific policy guidance, following the demise of the National Development Group, from IDC (the Independent Development Council for People with Mental Handicap) were helping to create a new vision of what local services might become.

In 1979 when the 'an ordinary life' initiative began, however, there was no well-documented British account of a comprehensive pattern of residential services which used ordinary housing. There were some small-scale projects beginning to put this idea to the test (of which the NIMROD project in South Glamorgan was then best known) but we had to look abroad for a *working* demonstration of what is possible – and here the achievements of ENCOR, the Eastern Nebraska Community Office of Retardation, seemed to offer particularly valuable lessons.

As a start to filling this gap, therefore, we convened the first working group to explore how local residential services reflecting key elements in the ENCOR model might be developed in the UK. The participants were drawn from voluntary agencies, health and local authorities and research groups in different parts of the country and all shared a deep interest in the ENCOR approach. As in much of the work which followed, we started with some appreciation of the enormous disadvantages experienced by many people with learning disabilities and some images of how things might be very different. In overcoming the deficiencies of past provision, we saw the importance of making explicit our commitment to three fundamental principles:

1) *People with learning disabilities have the same human value as anyone else and the same human rights.*

2) *Living like others within the community is both a right and a need.*

3) *Services must recognise the individuality of people with learning disabilities.*

We were keen to find practical ways of putting these principles into practice. Over a year we met regularly to put together information and advice for planners and providers on the design of residential services, leading to the first publication in the 'an ordinary life' series.

The working group intended that paper to be no more than a beginning. We recognised that if further progress was to be made in improving the opportunities available to people with learning disabilities, it was vital for workers in different places to come together to learn from each other's experiences and establish means of mutual support. We hoped it would be possible to refine and develop the ideas in *An Ordinary Life* and test them more fully in practice.

This indeed proved to be the case. A second edition was published two years later (King's Fund 1982) which has been re-printed three times and become widely known. Several hundred people participated in King's Fund conferences where its suggestions were explored and meetings were arranged in other parts of the country. In turn these discussions contributed to local service development activities which produced both new insights and an agenda of wider issues for the growing network of interested people to address. Thus the 'an ordinary life' initiative took shape.

As this work has developed, we have had to give fresh thought to the terms we employ. Words are important: they shape the ways we think and influence the ways we act. Labels are an essential tool for comprehension and communication. When labels are applied to people, however, they all too readily become a basis for stereotypes. In turn we may then respond to the stereotype rather than the whole person. Sadly, as the history of responses to people with learning disabilities shows only too clearly, the labels and stereotypes may become invested with derogatory meanings and the people put at further disadvantage.

Probably the wise course is to avoid labelling people whenever possible and to focus instead on each person's unique situation, wishes and needs. There are times, however – for example, in identifying the users of particular services – when some collective term is helpful. In earlier publications 'people with mental handicap' denoted our field of interest. We now think this label has disadvantages, not least because the people to whom it is applied seem very often to dislike it. In this book we refer instead to *people with learning disabilities*. We hope this term will encourage a concern with the person as someone with abilities as well as disabilities. The attention to disability should encourage us to take action, through support to individuals and changes in the environment, which reduces the experience of handicap. The focus on learning should suggest the importance of education in its broadest sense as the major form of assistance.

AN ORDINARY LIFE – STRATEGY AND INFLUENCE

The processes involved in the early years of the 'an ordinary life' initiative have been replicated and extended in subsequent work. Looking back we can trace the evolution of a strategy for promoting change which has involved eight main elements:

1) Working with local people at the forefront in planning and delivering community-based services to clarify the principles underpinning these services and produce detailed guidance on their design and development;

2) Linking with funding bodies (notably the Joseph Rowntree Memorial Trust) to encourage relevant action research and evaluation studies;

3) Publishing the results of this work in accessible form: *An Ordinary Life* has been followed by *An Ordinary Working Life, Facing the Challenge: an ordinary life for people with learning difficulties and challenging behaviour, An Ordinary Community Life*, two books and eleven other project papers (see Appendix I);

4) Using these publications as a vehicle for bringing people from different local services together to learn from each other's experiences and to establish mutual aid networks in different parts of the country;

5) Promoting the involvement of people with learning disabilities themselves in shaping local services and developing methods which facilitate this;

6) Drawing lessons from innovative services about the policies required to develop good services on a larger scale and working more intensively with authorities in particular areas to design and implement appropriate local strategies for change;

7) Linking with other independent national organisations (notably IDC, CMH and CMHERA – the Community and Mental Handicap Educational and Research Association) to widen the impact of all this work; and

8) Contributing directly and indirectly to discussion of the national policies required to promote high quality services everywhere.

These activities have led to widespread interest in this initiative and increasing local commitment to its philosophy over the last eight years. While we originally had to look abroad for 'working models' of new services, we now have evidence, if only on a small scale, of 'an ordinary life in practice'. As Ann Shearer reports in *Building Community* (1986)

> The component parts of the comprehensive community services of the future are slowly growing in more and more places. They are there in family support services and new opportunities for integrated education. They are there in the increasing use of ordinary housing by people with mental handicaps – and that includes people whose handicaps are very severe. They are there in the attempts to break down the bulk provision called 'day care' and offer people instead their chance to share in ordinary places of learning and work. They are there in the building of social networks and opportunities to enjoy ordinary leisure, without which 'community care' would be a bleak enough prospect for any of us.

These new services have shown a welcome openness to review and evaluation. We have been able to assess the benefits derived by their users – living, working and relaxing in improved surroundings, with greater personal dignity and more opportunities for access to ordinary community resources. We have been able to enlarge our understanding of the fundamental principles and give fresh emphasis to the importance of recognising that everyone, however severe the disability, is a developing person with his or her own contribution to make. We are also seeing an increase in momentum as statutory authorities, including the Welsh Office and a number of English regional health authorities (in collaboration with relevant local authorities), begin to implement large-scale strategies for change.

However, we are still at an early stage of a national transformation in services which presents formidable challenges. Although declining in size, most of the NHS institutions remain and further institutional provision is being created in many places. Naturally the pioneer community-based services are still developing the optimum ways of working and the achievements of even the best may remain insecure in the absence of strong support at senior levels in the providing agencies. There remains much to be learnt about ways of involving people with learning disabilities themselves in these services and about how best to widen their participation with non-disabled people in community activities. Work is required too on how these objectives can best be achieved in different circumstances including, for example,

communities with significant black and ethnic minority populations. There is also a major need for further investment in
fostering public understanding and involvement in improving
opportunities for people with learning disabilities.

While the increasing pace of change is welcome, this period of
opportunity is also a period of risk. Unless the development of
community-based services is managed with considerable skill and
continuing vigilance, the pressure for quick results may undermine the commitment to quality and weaken support among staff
and relatives as well as service users.

These problems are reinforced to the extent that financial
constraints raise further anxieties about the viability of good local
services. Some authorities are indeed backing their intentions
with appropriate resources but, as both the House of Commons
Social Services Committee (1985) and the Audit Commission
(1986) have pointed out, there remain significant doubts about
how far it will be possible to implement comprehensive local
services – for people living in the community as well as those
already in residential care – while also meeting the 'bridging' costs
involved in running old and new services in parallel. Government
policies in England remain complacent or ambiguous on these
questions and (for example, in the formal response to the Social
Services Committee Report 1985) appear strangely out of touch
with recent local innovations in philosophy and practice. At the
time of writing, it remains to be seen whether the current review
of these policies by Sir Roy Griffiths will pay proper attention to
issues of quality and coverage in the search for more rational
arrangements for organising and financing 'community care'.

All these issues provide challenges enough for the 'an ordinary
life' initiative in the next eight years.

THIS BOOK – STRUCTURE AND CONTENTS

All the contributors to this book have been involved – as service
users and advocates, local innovators and evaluators – in the
movement for 'an ordinary life' and have participated in the
King's Fund's own programme of work in support of this initiative.

Their contributions are organised into three parts. Part One
explores the foundations for developing high quality community-
based services. Paul Williams and Alan Tyne address the obvious
but crucial theme that implicit in any pattern of services is a set of
values defining the way people with learning disabilities are
expected to live. Their challenging message is that in the past,

and in much of what is still happening, people with learning disabilities have been treated in ways which add to their disadvantage. Positive action to redress this unfairness requires that all of us try to put ourselves in their place and make explicit the values we think should underpin the development of good services – values we would want applied to ourselves.

Chris Gathercole argues in Chapter 2 that empathy is not enough: it is high time we took seriously the need to involve people with learning disabilities directly in decisions about service provision. Such involvement is of course consistent with the much wider movement for consumer participation but difficulties have to be confronted honestly if the participative philosophy is to be translated into meaningful practice. To this end Chris suggests a wide variety of useful approaches.

In Part Two, more detailed attention is given to the implications of these values for the design and development of key elements in a comprehensive pattern of community-based services. Each of the seven chapters draws on experiences from some of the best of current efforts to implement 'an ordinary life' in different parts of the UK.

Philippa Russell begins by reviewing what has been learnt in recent years about a community approach to serving children with learning disabilities and their families. Philippa emphasises that these children should be seen as children first and that services must be sensitive to their individual needs and family situation. Good services start from a commitment to partnership with parents and require effective arrangements for inter-professional and inter-agency collaboration which should continue as the child grows into adolescence and adulthood.

In Chapter 4, Ritchard Brazil and Nan Carle return to the origins of 'an ordinary life' and examine why an ordinary home life is so important. Through descriptions of innovative services in London they explore ways in which public and voluntary agencies can tackle the organisational problems involved in providing residential services which allow individual users a choice of housing options.

Linda Ward argues in Chapter 5 that even good residential services are only a starting point on the way to enabling individuals to enjoy a fuller life in the community. Drawing particularly on experience from community support services developed in Bristol, Linda provides a detailed illustration of the contribution which opportunities for integration, either fostered by services or (more importantly), by members of the local community, can make to the quality of people's lives.

The integration of people with learning disabilities is also the focus of Chapter 6, where Jan Porterfield argues that more and more of them want real jobs and many, given appropriate support, could get them. From a review of the growing number of innovative employment schemes across the country, Jan identifies essential lessons for further local initiatives.

In considering each of these aspects of provision, Chapters 4, 5 and 6 emphasise the importance of examining the impact of services on the lives of individuals. Indeed, each chapter presents a pen-picture of people with learning disabilities known to the authors. As Chris Gathercole argues in Chapter 2, this concern with individual experience must be reflected in much wider efforts to enable people to speak for themselves. In Chapter 7, Alice Etherington, Keven Hall and Emma Whelan, who have significant experience as users of existing services, provide accounts of how they live their lives, their sources of support and their aspirations for the future. Retracing the topics of preceding chapters, Alice, Keven and Emma give particular attention to home life, work and leisure activities and the opportunities these offer for making and maintaining friendships.

Janet Maher and Oliver Russell consider in Chapter 8 how best to serve the small numbers of people in any locality who, for a variety of reasons, behave in ways which produce despair among those who care for them and whose needs for affection may be difficult to supply. Starting from the belief that all people with learning disabilities can live in the community given appropriate resources, Janet and Oliver draw on their own work in Bristol to describe the design of services for people with very challenging behaviour.

Completing Part Two, Roger Blunden argues the importance not only of developing good services but also of investing in explicit efforts to maintain standards and build in the capacity for making further improvements in the light of experience. Drawing both on the IDC's (1986) proposals for pursuing quality and ideas about 'excellence' from the business world, he describes a systematic approach to assessing and safeguarding quality.

Part Three takes up the issues involved in reproducing comprehensive local services consistent with the principles of 'an ordinary life' on a large scale. Many of the most impressive examples of current service provision (like those described in *Building Community*) have developed incrementally and initially on a small scale through the energy, ingenuity and commitment of innovative groups – sometimes despite, rather than because of, the approaches adopted more widely in local agencies. However, recent years have seen a shift from this pattern of 'project' growth towards the adoption of more radical strategies designed to secure rapid development in services to whole districts, counties or even regions. Drawing on experience in three of the more forward-looking English regions, Chapters 10, 11 and 12 examine how important issues in achieving large-scale change can be addressed.

In Chapter 10, Chris Gathercole, Tom McLean and David Whalley describe how, over many years, pioneering efforts to improve the quality of life for residents in a large hospital have contributed to the evolution of a purposeful strategy for the North West as a whole which will ultimately make such hospitals redundant. They emphasise the ways in which growing commitment to revaluing people with learning disabilities and continuing efforts to learn how to do better have been reflected in widespread local action.

In Chapter 11 these themes are explored further with specific attention to training for service development. Using examples from imaginative initiatives under way in the South East Thames region, Jim Mansell argues for a broad approach to staff training which promotes organisational change as well as improving individual competence and which seeks to bridge planning and implementation.

Finally, drawing particularly on work with health and local authorities in the South West of England, I examine the dilemmas involved in working through large public bureaucracies to implement multi-agency services which are sensitively tailored to individual wishes and needs. In particular I consider the leadership required at strategic levels in these authorities if the momentum towards 'an ordinary life in practice' is to be sustained.

$$* \quad * \quad *$$

If these accounts offer some encouragement, all the contributors recognise that this is only a start in the efforts which will be required to offer people with learning disabilities the opportunities and support needed to enjoy normal patterns of life within the community. At the King's Fund work towards this aim continues: Roger Blunden, Joan Rush and Andrea Whittaker at the King's Fund Centre are addressing further issues in the design of services which promote maximum opportunities for integration; at the King's Fund College Ritchard Brazil and Nan Carle are increasing our assistance to field authorities confronting the challenges of planning and implementing large-scale change; at the King's Fund Institute, these and other staff from across the Fund are engaged in an independent study of the national policies required in response to the Audit Commission critique. As with all the work to date, further progress depends on widening the networks of people engaged in local initiatives and learning from each other's experiences. Fundamentally this book is an invitation to join these endeavours – to take action with others for 'an ordinary life'.

David Towell

References

Audit Commission (1986) Making a reality of community care. London, HMSO.

Blunden R and Allen D (eds) 1987 Facing the challenge: an ordinary life for people with learning difficulties and challenging behaviour (project paper 74). London, King Edward's Hospital Fund for London.

Department of Health and Social Security (1985) Government response to the second report from the social services com‐ mittee, 1984–5 session: Community care with special reference to adult mentally ill and mentally handicapped people. Cmnd 9674. London, HMSO.

House of Commons (1985) Community care with special ref‐ erence to adult mentally ill and mentally handicapped people. Second report from the social services committee, sessions 1984–5. Volume I. London, HMSO.

Independent Development Council for People with Mental Handicap (1986) Pursuing quality: how good are your local services for people with mental handicap? London, IDC.

King's Fund (1980) An ordinary life: comprehensive locally-based residential services for mentally handicapped people (project paper 24). London, King Edward's Hospital Fund for London.

King's Fund (1982) An ordinary life: comprehensive locally-based residential services for mentally handicapped people (project paper 24) (second edition). London, King Edward's Hospital Fund for London.

King's Fund (1984) An ordinary working life: vocational services for people with mental handicap (project paper 50). London, King Edward's Hospital Fund for London.

King's Fund (forthcoming) An ordinary community life. London, King Edward's Hospital Fund for London.

Parliament (1979) Report of the committee of enquiry into mental handicap nursing and care. Cmnd 7468. London, HMSO. (Chairman Peggy Jay.)

Shearer A (1986) Building community with people with mental handicap, their families and friends. London, Campaign for People with Mental Handicaps and King Edward's Hospital Fund for London.

Part One

REVALUING PEOPLE WITH LEARNING DISABILITIES

Paul Williams and Alan Tyne

Exploring values as the basis for service development

How much does society value people with learning disabilities? Do we value them enough to want them to enjoy and benefit from the same sorts of activities, relationships and experiences as others? Do we value them enough to want to invest the right kind and amount of support to help them to do so?

If we ask these last two questions of ourselves as *individuals*, the answers will often be 'yes'. Many of us value people with disabilities highly and apply those values in relationships and activities with them. However, applying these questions to the beliefs and behaviour of society as a whole, reflected in the nature of services and social treatment of people with disabilities generally, shows a very different picture.

Though we as individuals may value people with disabilities as friends, neighbours or colleagues, as workers, and as adults equal to ourselves, society as a whole has, throughout history, tended to regard them as a menace or a nuisance, as objects of ridicule or pity and charity, as less than fully human, as sick, or as eternal children (Wolfensberger 1972, 1975).

Since social values determine the shape of services, individual members of staff often find themselves in a difficult and para-doxical situation. They may wish to apply their positive personal values, but they work in service systems whose nature is deter-mined by negative social values.

We can clearly see the operation of different social values in different countries and at different times in history. For example, many of the large institutions we still have with us in Britain and other parts of Europe, and in the USA, have their origins in the eugenics movement of the early 20th century, when it was believed that if the 'feebleminded' were allowed to breed, they would have more children than other people and those children would all have disabilities and criminal propensities; a higher and higher proportion of the population would become disabled, the ability of the whole nation would drop, and criminality and moral degeneracy would be rampant. Institutions were therefore deliberately built to segregate people with disabilities from society and to separate the sexes within the institutions themselves (Wolfensberger 1975).

On the other hand, there have been times when very positive values have asserted themselves. During the 1950s and early 60s there was great optimism in this country about the potential of people with severe learning disabilities to work. One of us, for example, as a student in the 1960s under the guidance of Professor Jack Tizard, carried out a study of how a man with profound learning disabilities was taught to work on an industrial task in an adult training centre (Williams 1967). In parts of the USA, they are still optimistic about work possibilities even for people with very severe learning disabilities, and pioneer work has been carried out by Tom Bellamy (Bellamy *et al* 1979). Over the last decade in Britain we seem rather to have lost sight of that ideal in our development of what we call 'social education', and a strong interest in work has only recently begun to be revived (King's Fund 1984).

Today we are rather equivocal in our attitudes towards people with learning disabilities. We are slowly moving towards provision of ordinary housing but retain well-rehearsed rationales for keeping segregated provision. Voluntary organisations cannot decide whether to portray people with learning disabilities as equal citizens with equal rights (*cf* some of the Spastics Society's current publicity) or as poor pathetic creatures deserving of pity and charity (*cf* MENCAP's 'little Stephen' posters, advertisements and logo).

DEVALUING EXPERIENCES

The consequences of the operation of negative social values represent additional handicaps that are superimposed on a person's basic disabilities. The prevalence of the following experiences for people with disabilities is proof of the continuing operation of very negative social values.

Rejection from local services and agencies, schools, work opportunities, housing or accommodation, clubs, organisations and leisure facilities.

Physical segregation Many are taken away from their own neighbourhoods and are placed in settings that are apart from ordinary communities or are geographically remote and isolated.

Isolation from socially valued people They often spend most of their lives in the company of others like them and have few opportunities to meet other people.

Lack of roots   Because they often live in places apart from the communities where they grew up or where their families live, and because they are often moved between different residences, they may have great difficulty in retaining roots in a particular place.

Lack of relationships   They may spend most of their time with people who find it difficult to form relationships and have very few opportunities to meet people other than staff, who may change quite frequently.

Insecurity   Many live in places with poor physical security, where they may be subject to interference from other people or their property broken or stolen.

Lack of freedom and control   Generally, they have little control over their lives, and their freedom to move about or to do the things they wish to do is often severely curtailed.

Poverty   Most are materially poor, certainly when compared with people valued by society.

Lack of experience and opportunity   They are often overprotected and may miss out completely on important chances for development and growth.

Attribution of negative characteristics by association   A confused public image of people with disabilities is not helped by the tendency to group large numbers of them together. Individuals are associated with people with quite different disabilities or problems.

'Symbolic marking'   They tend to be surrounded by symbols or images which signal to the outside world that they are odd or different.

Ill-treatment   Regrettably, a number of inquiries and reports have testified to their physical ill-treatment.

Awareness of being a burden to others   Some may have spent their lives being spoken of by others in negative terms, as a problem or a nuisance.

Having one's life wasted   Compared with people who are valued by society, their lives, through no choice of their own, are often

25

wasted. Little opportunity is offered to them to make any contribution to ordinary society, either through their activities or their relationships.

If we accept that people with disabilities often have a lifetime of negative experiences due to the operation of negative social values, especially in service provision, what can be done to improve their lives?

REDRESSING DISADVANTAGE

We believe that the answer is to adopt a 'value-based' approach. 'Value-based' in this context means the application of exactly the same values that are applied to others in society. Furthermore, because the experiences of many people with disabilities have been so bad, extremely high standards are needed in order to compensate. People with disabilities are not 'just like other people': they have been deprived and discriminated against systematically and need positive compensatory action (Wolfensberger and Thomas 1983).

There are two essential steps in the adoption of the 'value-based' approach. First, an accurate and empathic understanding of the experiences undergone by those with disabilities is required. Second, agreement on a specific set of values to be applied in service provision must be sought.

To achieve the first of these, we begin all our training work with an exercise in which we ask people to review the life of someone they know who has learning disabilities and compare it with their own. Sometimes it emerges that very little is known of their subject's history; there may be gaps of several years or even decades for which no records or memories are accessible. Usually, however, many stark contrasts between that person's life and their own appear. The exercise thus leads to a greater appreciation of the reality behind many of the negative experiences listed earlier.

Although people often find this exercise difficult and painful, there is no substitute for it. Attempts to opt out of doing it by claiming not to know anyone with disabilities well enough or by simply regurgitating clinical case-notes defeat the purpose. The essence lies in trying to imagine key experiences in the other's life and empathising with their feelings.

Start the exercise by listing your subject's life history as far as you know it, concentrating on key events: birth, starting school, taking part in local activities, perhaps being admitted to residential care or the death of a parent. Consider the choices and opportunities which would have been available at each stage. Beside this, list the life story of a socially valued person (maybe yourself). Is there a difference? How great is the contrast?

The second step in the adoption of a value-based approach is to reach agreement on a list of important values that almost everyone in our society would regard as highly positive and would like to have applied to themselves.

This will obviously include a wide range of situations and experiences. The intention, however, is not to be prescriptive (we could not and should not envisage the writing of reference manuals to tell us how people should be treated) but to identify the experiences or situations that practically nobody would value as well as those which are valued by most people (O'Brien and Tyne 1981).

It is relatively easy to identify those aspects of the lives of people with disabilities – such as living on a hospital ward – that we would consider to be unpleasant or undesirable. The first part of this chapter included a catalogue of these.

The list below is an attempt to identify some of the things that practically everyone is likely to value.

- having easy physical access to a wide range of people and places
- not living in close proximity to large numbers of people who are likely to be seen as 'odd'
- having a good reputation
- having lots of opportunity to meet people
- being treated as an adult, with corresponding freedoms and responsibilities
- not being made to seem 'odd' or negatively different
- having intensive help to overcome any disabilities or disadvantages
- comfortable settings to live or work in
- being treated as an individual
- being respected and treated well
- being served by organisations and programmes that have the structures and supports to enable all these things to happen and be maintained.

Once we have such a list, we can identify specific aspects of services that constitute good or bad practice in the application of these values. We have assembled many illustrations on slides for use in our own teaching.

EVALUATING PERFORMANCE

There is an evaluation instrument designed to measure how successfully these values are being applied in services. It is known as programme analysis of service systems (PASS) and was developed in the 1970s in the USA by Professor W Wolfensberger. We use it extensively in our own training work to teach people the importance of values in services and to help them to understand the detailed implications of a value-based approach (Wolfensberger and Glenn 1975).

The PASS instrument is a comprehensive manual of issues and standards. When used by a visiting team making detailed observations, scores or indices of service quality in several key areas are obtained. Access and avoidance of congregation are covered in a score representing suitability of *location*. The images conveyed by the building, and its comfort, are covered in a score representing adequacy of *appearance*. The help given to people in achieving a good reputation, meeting people, overcoming handicaps, and not seeming 'odd' or negatively different, and the respect accorded to them as adults and as individuals, are covered in a score representing the quality of the *programme*. The existence of structures and supports to enable good quality services to be developed and maintained is covered in a score representing effectiveness of *administration*.

At the Community and Mental Handicap Educational and Research Association (CMHERA), which has been responsible for the introduction of PASS-based teaching in Britain, we have prepared an analysis of the assessed performance on PASS of over 100 services. These range from large institutions to small community-based services and include day and residential services run by a range of agencies for people with a wide variety of disabilities.

Much of the data has been collected by students in introductory workshops based on PASS; the validity of the judgments made is thus open to doubt. However, the results strongly indicate that, from the value-based perspective of PASS, there are many serious problems and drawbacks with most service patterns developed in the past as well as those being developed today (Williams 1987a, 1987b). As just one example, adult training centres run by social services departments are shown to be very unsatisfactory in the way they isolate and segregate people, and fail to provide adequate conditions for effective learning or enhancement of social status.

In residential services, many service patterns that have been tried as alternatives to traditional large institutions are shown to be unacceptable: flats or bungalows in hospital grounds, large 'hostels' run by health authorities or social services departments, 'village communities' run by voluntary organisations, privatised institutions and so on.

The only residential services shown to offer a promising physical base for pursuing value-based principles are those using ordinary housing which follow the guidelines and recommendations of *An Ordinary Life* (King's Fund 1982). However, our limited use of PASS indicates that these improvements are largely confined to the areas of *location* and *appearance*.

Practice in the area of *programme* – helping people to achieve a good reputation, meet others, overcome their handicaps, not be seen as unnecessarily 'odd', and treating them with respect as adults and individuals – has been disappointing. 'Life-sharing' situations where people with and without learning disabilities share their living space and daily activities are exceptions, but they are rare and certainly do not constitute the model we seem to be pursuing in current service developments.

A clear implication is that the 'life-sharing' model should be studied more closely, and that ways need to be developed of recruiting, training and supporting people to successfully adopt this role.

The section of PASS concerned with *administration* includes some items which derive from a value-based ideology, for example relating to policies promoting the use of generic services; development of comprehensive local service structures which do not exclude people from integrative local resources; and the involvement of service users and the general public in decisions and management.

Other items included relate to good administrative practice in any efficient organisation, for example staff training, service evaluation, effective planning processes, staff renewal and avoidance of 'burnout', and effective management control structures.

Practice in these areas is shown by our PASS-based studies to be unacceptably poor in all services. This is particularly serious in the case of services based on ordinary houses or involving 'life-sharing', since they may be very fragile, insecure and vulnerable without strong and supportive management and administration. A priority of all service development, especially value-based service development, would therefore seem to be the creation of better support arrangements.

29

These findings show clearly that we are only just beginning to explore the implications of a value-based approach in services (Tyne 1987a, 1987b). We strongly believe, however, that this approach represents an essential philosophical underpinning for current and future pioneer service developments, such as those described later in this book, if they are to be successful in improving the lives of people with learning disabilities.

Acknowledgments

The ideas in this paper derive from the work and thought of Wolf Wolfensberger of Syracuse University, New York, especially as developed and taught to us by John O'Brien of Responsive Systems Associates, Georgia, USA. Our pursuit of the ideas in Britain is only possible with the help of a network of colleagues who assist us in our teaching, advisory and evaluation work. During much of its development we were supported by a grant from the Joseph Rowntree Memorial Trust. Parts of this chapter are based on papers given by Paul Williams to a conference on 'Evaluating quality of care', organised by the British Institute of Mental Handicap and held in Nottingham in July 1986, and to the Thirteenth Annual Congress of the Association of Professions for Mentally Handicapped People, held at Lancaster University, also in July 1986.

References

Bellamy GT, Horner RH and Inman DP (1979) Vocational habilitation of severely retarded adults. Baltimore, University Park Press.

King's Fund (1982) An ordinary life: comprehensive locally-based residential services for mentally handicapped people (project paper 24). London, King Edward's Hospital Fund for London.

King's Fund (1984) An ordinary working life: vocational services for people with mental handicap (project paper 50). London, King Edward's Hospital Fund for London.

O'Brien J and Tyne A (1981) The principle of normalisation: a foundation for effective services. London, Campaign for People with Mental ·Handicaps.

Tyne A (1987a) Some practical dilemmas and strategies in values-led approaches to change. In: Ward L (ed). Getting better all the time? Issues and strategies for ensuring quality in community services for people with mental handicap (project paper 66). London, King Edward's Hospital Fund for London.

Tyne A (1987b) Shaping community services – the impact of an idea. In: Malin N (ed). Reassessing community care. London, Croom Helm.

Williams P (1967) Industrial training and remunerative employment of the profoundly retarded. British Journal of Mental Subnormality 13: 14–23.

Williams P (1987a) Evaluating services from the consumer's point of view. In: Zadik T and Beswick J (eds). Evaluating quality of care. Kidderminster, British Institute of Mental Handicap.

Williams P (1987b) Value-based training and service change. In: Our lives, your jobs: proceedings of the Thirteenth Annual Congress of the Association of Professions for Mentally Handicapped People. Ross-on-Wye, APMH.

Wolfensberger W (ed) (1972) The principle of normalisation in human services. Toronto, National Institute on Mental Retardation.

Wolfensberger W (1975) The origin and nature of our institutional models. Syracuse, Human Policy Press.

Wolfensberger W and Glenn L (1975) PASS – programme analysis of service systems (3rd edition). Toronto, National Institute on Mental Retardation.

Wolfensberger W and Thomas S (1983) PASSING – programme analysis of service systems' implementation of normalisation goals. Toronto, National Institute on Mental Retardation.

Chris Gathercole

Involving people with learning disabilities

Involvement implies contributing, sharing some activity, being listened to and having one's views respected, perhaps with the possibility of influencing decisions. Traditionally, of course, people with learning disabilities have been seen as passive recipients of services. The suggestion that they might have a say in how services are developed and run is very recent. Its novelty has caught everyone· unprepared. This chapter explores recent attempts to enable service users to influence services and examines the kinds of local action which will improve user participation.

The demand for increased participation has created a significant movement in the past 20 years: consumers of public services such as railways and telephones through user councils, GPs' patients through patient participation groups, health service users through community health councils, parents and pupils on boards of governors of schools, council house tenants through tenants' associations and workers through industrial democracy (Richardson 1983). It is significant that it is only now that the possibility of participation by people with learning disabilities is being raised.

Anyone who is concerned about the lives of people with learning disabilities should have opportunities to be involved in improving services. This includes service users, their relatives, staff, managers, planners, policy makers, volunteers, friends, advocates and public representatives such as Members of Parliament and local councillors. Much of what follows applies to all interested parties but the focus of the discussion will be on people with learning disabilities as service users.

Although there is much lip service paid to the idea of involving consumers, very little actually seems to happen. There are workers' councils in some adult training centres, based on self-advocacy. Some hospitals have residents represented on their various committees. Users occasionally participate with staff in training events, especially those on normalisation. Sometimes users make contributions at conferences describing their experiences. However, despite the rhetoric, the extent of consumer participation is very limited. Users of services exert minimal influence over service development. The balance needs to be redressed (Brandon and Brandon 1987).

FIVE BENEFITS OF USER PARTICIPATION

1 The involvement of consumers in planning and governing increases the likelihood that a service will be responsive to their needs. Since users have a personal investment in the quality of the service they receive, that service is more likely to be effective. Even if they were to say nothing, their very presence, when decisions are being taken, is a reminder of whom the service is intended to serve.

2 In a democratic society, a high value is placed on the right of people to be involved in decisions which affect their lives. It is regarded as only just, therefore, that those most affected by a service should be involved in its design and operation. If they are not, then there is a greater likelihood of the service serving the needs of staff rather than users.

3 Planners do not have all the information needed on which to base the best decisions. Service users are valuable reservoirs of knowledge and experience which should be included in service planning, development and operation.

4 A responsive and adaptive service system needs people at all levels to have a hand in guiding it along. Increased community living will inevitably cause some untoward events. User involvement increases the likelihood of problems coming to light so they can be dealt with promptly. Without involvement there are serious dangers that community care will deteriorate. The worst things can happen in the name of high ideals unless there are safeguards for basic standards. User involvement is one way of ensuring that services damage people as little as possible.

5 Enabling users to participate contributes to major service accomplishments by showing respect for people, increasing their control over their lives, extending their relationships and helping them learn to live with others.

SOME WAYS OF INVOLVING SERVICE USERS

There is a great variety of formal and informal ways in which users can influence decisions, all of which should be encouraged. Some involve face-to-face contact between users and decision-makers, while others, such as surveys, do not. Different levels of involvement can be distinguished, from matters concerning one person's future to the wider scene where matters affecting many users are considered, as in district planning. Different degrees of influence over decisions and their implementation can be distinguished, from zero to token consultation through to full control. In Figure 1, some of the methods to be discussed are illustrated on a graph using these two variables (level of involvement and degree of user influence) as axes.

At the simplest level services should make information more readily available to users. This can be done through professional reports being given to them so that they can gain a better understanding of their own situation and what they can do about it. It can be done at the wider level by making information about services and plans for change more public. Government in this country is traditionally very secretive. Being more open gives users more opportunities to learn what they need to do to make their contribution.

Personal contact with policy makers, planners and senior administrators who are often remote from the grassroots can help foster mutual understanding. This requires those with much influence to make themselves available and those with little influence to learn whom to contact and how. It might be through some common interest, such as church membership or perhaps by invitation to tea at home.

The self-advocacy movement is calling attention to the need for people with disabilities to be free to speak up for themselves. Contributing to the formulation of individual programme plans (IPPs) can have an influence beyond one's own personal life, for example through service deficiency reports and IPP reviews in which managers consider wider implications of IPP recommendations. Through group activities such as the People First movement, views can be disseminated through newsletters and conference resolutions.

Using complaints procedures, consumers can often have more influence than they realise, by drawing the attention of managers to service problems. This can take some courage as many people are reluctant to face up to authority.

People who have difficulty speaking up for themselves can benefit from having someone else, who may be a relative or a friend who is an ordinary citizen, to represent their interests. This might be at individual level as in citizen advocacy (Carle 1984) or on a wider scale as in collective advocacy (Wolfensberger 1977).

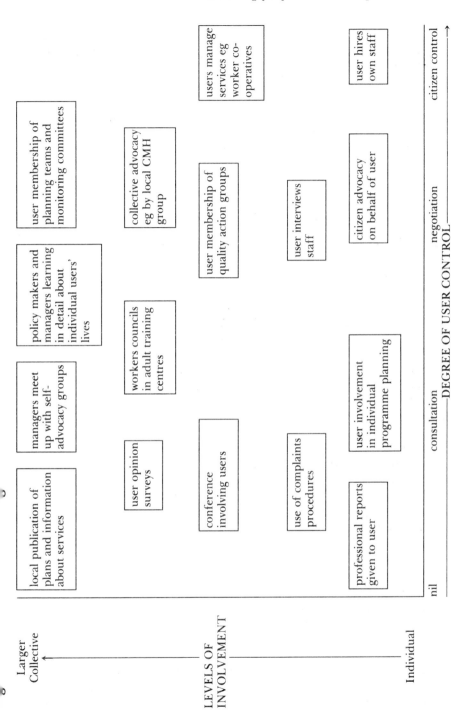

Community health councils, the Campaign for People with Mental Handicaps (CMH), Royal MENCAP and the Spastics Society all take on this latter role.

Service providers can do systematic surveys of consumer views, using individual interviews (Wandsworth 1976) and group discussions such as search conferences (Emery 1982). This might be done by the research section of a social services department, by students on basic professional training courses, by independent researchers from universities or by consumer groups themselves.

Outside the service setting staff and users can come together as equal partners in joint activities like the CMH participation events (Shearer 1972, 1973; CMH 1975).

Users and staff can learn together as equal participants in training events such as workshops on normalisation. Users can contribute to staff training as well as conferences by describing their experiences and what they want in life. Planners and policy makers can learn what life is like for users of services through 'getting to know you' workshops (Brost and Johnson 1982) in which each participant spends some time getting to know a person with a learning disability.

Users could be members of service evaluation teams such as the quality action groups recommended by the Independent Development Council (IDC 1986).

Places can be reserved for users on advisory committees which can act as watchdogs:

> Each geographic team of Eleanor Roosevelt Development Services, which serves a population from 50,000 to 150,000, has a consumer board comprising representatives from the consumer agencies and individuals in its catchment area. ... Individuals with handicaps, parents of institutionalised children and adults, and staff representatives from community agencies and public schools are important members of the consumer boards. The boards meet with staff at least monthly to discuss and act upon program planning, implementation, and evaluation. They also advise the staff on priorities, assist in community education, and assume responsibility. (NIMR 1978)

Membership of various committees, working parties and task forces can provide a vehicle for influence. Membership of staff appointment panels is particularly appropriate where staff will have considerable direct contact with a user.

More radically, it is possible to envisage arrangements which directly empower users – current examples of which are mainly evident in services for people with physical disabilities – through enabling users to hire their own staff or establishing employment situations which are run as worker cooperatives.

SOME DANGERS

Despite the consensus that participation is a good thing, there are dangers which should be recognised, mostly to do with perversions of high ideals in practice. Participation may be seen by those holding power as a way of legitimising existing power relationships through tokenism. Users are co-opted, thus reducing their effectiveness as an independent voice through their involvement in enervating bureaucratic delay. If not experienced in committee procedures and the ways of bureaucracy, users may be manipulated to serve the ends of people other than those supposedly served by the service. They will often need support and guidance to learn how to make the most effective contribution. If such support is not forthcoming, they may be dismissed as not worth bothering with. Then there is the enthusiastic decision maker who does not understand the limitations of people who have not had the chance to make choices in their lives and does not make adequate support available to enable them to learn.

Another serious danger is that others who may be concerned to take a stand alongside vulnerable people may feel they have to withdraw in order to leave users to promote their own interests. This would in effect be abandoning people who are oppressed, who have very little power and few resources. It is vitally important that those with greater influence and resources use their power to defend people with learning disabilities and show solidarity with their cause.

The role of adviser to self-advocacy groups is a particularly difficult one. Pressure on users to conform to the adviser's views would be very difficult to avoid. Even more problematic is whether prompting people dispersed throughout a community to come together may not be a subtle form of congregation and segregation.

While self-advocacy is to be supported, it should be recognised that it is likely to be a very limited safeguard and that other safeguards are needed to complement it. The voice of people with learning difficulties is not strong and will often be ignored. Even people claiming to be in favour of self-advocacy often do not listen. Others more powerful and influential will need to stand alongside them if their voice is to be heard.

SOME DIFFICULTIES IN INVOLVING SERVICE USERS

If genuine participation is to become a reality we need to examine where the difficulties lie. Then we will get a better idea as to what needs to be done to remedy the situation. Some difficulties are to do with those now holding power, some are to do with those denied power and some to do with both.

Since there is little tradition of consumer involvement in services for people with learning disabilities, people may not know where to start. As with anything new there may be a reluctance to take what seems like a step into the unknown. There may be a lack of openness and trust arising from our social traditions of 'us' and 'them', the adversarial stance. People may not appreciate the benefits of involving everyone who has a legitimate interest. Both parties may be mutually handicapped, not knowing how to relate to each other as equal partners: listening, contributing, negotiating. They may have different perceptions and expectations of the aims of consumer involvement and how this may best be achieved. Such differences may not be acknowledged and explicit but, if they exist, will certainly lead to tensions and conflict.

Those with influence may be reluctant to include service users in decision making because they consider that they really do know what is best. If they consider themselves as experts they may not want what they see as naive users disrupting the smooth flow of their plans. They would see involving users as taking time and unnecessarily delaying decisions. Bottom up planning is often not appreciated by those at the top of the service pyramid because they fear loss of their influence and control. This arises from the low expectations of those with influence who may not have realised what service users might contribute.

The power holders may be worried that they could not cope with what they would see as the extra demands on them arising from greater user involvement. Even if they were committed to the idea of consumer involvement, those with power may not know how to discover the views of consumers and the variety of ways in which users could participate.

In looking at the difficulties users may have in making their contribution, caution is needed to avoid 'blaming the victims'. They may not have a clear idea about what kind of services they would like. This could be because they have not been given the information they need. As victims of prejudice, they may see their own needs and the services they require in ways which could be considered damaging to their interests. They may have little experience of forming opinions, with others often making choices on their behalf. Through lack of experience they may not know how to coordinate their efforts and pilot their way through the system. They may be limited in the social skills and confidence needed. Formulating a case and presenting it requires skills in communication which they may need to develop. Someone with a disability may lack the energy needed for campaigning in addition to that needed for just getting through the day. Resources of time and money may be short. Having had little experience of challenging authority, users may be afraid to participate, worried that they will be marked out as trouble-makers and denied services.

WHAT CAN BE DONE TO IMPROVE PARTICIPATION?

The first stage in bringing about social change is for people to see the need for the change. Discussion is needed to draw attention to the importance of involving consumers and the benefits of doing so (Harper and Dobson 1985). It is an issue which has to be on everyone's agenda. Opportunities are needed to discuss the dangers and difficulties so that people become aware of the pitfalls and barriers.

Since involving consumers means that all parties concerned will be learning in the process, a commitment to learning will be a great help. It will therefore be highly desirable to explore the widest possible range of ways of involving consumers in order to learn as much as possible about how to do it effectively. Progress with one approach will inform other approaches whereas difficulties with any one approach won't bring the whole endeavour to a standstill.

The development requirements of the various parties involved should be carefully considered. Holders of power may need to learn to listen, while users of services may need to learn about the ways of committees and bureaucracies and how to make their views known.

At every level an example can be set by doing it. Participation events could be held, complaints procedures publicised, assertiveness training supported, self-advocacy, citizen advocacy and collective advocacy welcomed and encouraged, representation on committees and working parties actively sought, opinion surveys promoted and users involved in training events and quality action groups.

From time to time a review of progress could be held to identify what lessons have been learned and what difficulties remain and to celebrate the good things that have happened. Occasional reflection of this kind will help identify what local opportunities are available to develop user participation. This in turn will help to clarify the priorities for the next stage so that effort is focused and not dissipated unproductively.

A CHECKLIST FOR ACTION

In order to develop effective action locally some thought has to be given to a number of questions. Below are some useful starting points. It is unlikely that one person will be able to answer all of these questions so it would be useful to recruit perhaps eight or ten people from a variety of backgrounds to pool their knowledge.

What is happening now?

In what ways and to what extent are users participating in service development and governance?
What support are they receiving for participating?
Is their participation welcomed or made difficult?
What difficulties are these efforts meeting?
How could existing efforts be strengthened?
Who is committed to promoting participation?
Are the benefits widely recognised?

Resources

What help could be drawn on to facilitate users' social skills? (For example, is assertiveness training available through the women's movement?)
Who could run a 'getting to know you' workshop?
Who could be recruited to do surveys of users' opinions on various aspects of services?
Who can advise on the issues involved in getting citizen advocacy and collective advocacy going?
What organisations might be relevant in promoting user involvement? (For example, community health council, local authority tenants' association, ratepayers' association, GP's patients participation group.)
Who can be invited to facilitate user participation? (For example, community workers, adult education staff, housing welfare staff.)

Bringing about change

What would have to happen for the benefits to be more generally understood so that participation is more widely welcomed and promoted and who would this activity be aimed towards?

What training do staff need to facilitate user involvement in individual programme planning?

What would have to happen for users to be brought into local planning structures?

How could a participation event (as described by CMH) be arranged?

How could complaints procedures be publicised and their use encouraged?

What other questions do you need to ask to orientate effective action?

References

Brandon A and Brandon D (1987) Consumers as colleagues. London, MIND.

Brost M and Johnson T (1982) Getting to know you: one approach to service assessment and planning for individuals with disabilities. Madison, Wisconsin Coalition for Advocacy.

Carle N (1984) Key concepts in community based services. London, Campaign for People with Mental Handicaps.

CMH (1975) Working out. London, Campaign for People with Mental Handicaps.

Emery M (1982) Searching – for new directions – in new ways – for new times. Canberra, Centre for Continuing Education, Australian National University.

Harper G and Dobson J (1985) Participation: report of a workshop involving people with mental handicaps and staff who work with them. London, Campaign for People with Mental Handicaps.

IDC (1986) Pursuing quality – how good are your local services for people with mental handicap? London, Independent Development Council for People with Mental Handicap.

NIMR (1978) Residential services. Toronto, National Institute on Mental Retardation.

Richardson A (1983) Participation. London, Routledge and Kegan Paul.

Shearer A (1972) Our Life. London, Campaign for People with Mental Handicaps.

Shearer A (1973) Listen. London, Campaign for People with Mental Handicaps.
Wandsworth Social Services (1976) Project 74: a research study in which mentally handicapped people speak for themselves. London, Borough of Wandsworth.
Wolfensberger W (1977) A multi-component advocacy protection schema. Toronto, National Institute on Mental Retardation.

—————— Part Two ——————

DESIGNING, DEVELOPING AND
SAFEGUARDING HIGH QUALITY SERVICES

Philippa Russell

A community approach
to serving children and their families

What does it mean to this person to have this handicap;
At this time in his or her life;
With these care-givers;
In this environment;
In this locality;
With this peer group;
And with these professionals?

Joan Bicknell, *Right from the Start* (1981)

The birth of any child can be a frightening as well as a happy event for the family concerned. Parenthood brings new responsibilities and concerns, as well as pleasures. When the new baby has a learning disability or any special need, the initial diagnosis may devastate the parents. Research by Cunningham and Davis (1985a) and others clearly demonstrates the need to recognise the impact of disability on parental expectations and self-image – but confirms that active support and appropriate services can dramatically improve parental acceptance of and enjoyment in their child. As Hewett noted in 1970, 'the general tendency to characterise parents of handicapped children as guilt-ridden, anxiety laden ... over-protective and rejecting beings' is a reflection not of real feelings and attitudes but of the absence of coherent local practical support which gives dignity, respect and appropriate services to the whole family when a child has a learning disability or other special needs.*

Since 1970, major shifts in opinion have led to parents being perceived as 'partners' and as having not only a voice but direct skills to utilise in meeting their child's special needs. Recent

---

* This chapter follows the convention adopted throughout the book of using 'learning disabilities' in preference to 'mental handicap' or other designations. In the context of services to children, particularly since the 1981 Education Act, this convention requires some qualification. A note on definitions is included at the end of the chapter.

studies (Cunningham and Davis 1985b) emphasise the importance of professionals as well as parents in perceiving a child with learning disabilities as a child first, and disabled second. Government reports from Court (Parliament 1976) and Warnock (Parliament 1978) emphasise the duality of parents and professionals and the importance of developing a dialogue which offers parity of esteem between service providers and family consumers. A genuinely multi-disciplinary service will focus upon the whole family. It will be based upon policies which maximise parental involvement and skill sharing, with integration into mainstream children's services wherever possible. Many traditional services for children with learning disabilities have failed to facilitate the normal experience of parenting because of the absence of a focus on good quality child care. The same services have often ignored the psychological and social aspects of disability within a family. Childhood offers an opportunity to initiate ongoing assessment: to involve families rather than exclude them and to initiate a continuum of care based within an agreed framework for mutual support between parents and professionals. Collaborative planning and goal setting is a problem in adult services. Many children's services already liaise effectively and legislation such as the 1981 Education Act and the forthcoming DHSS child care law review offer challenges (and opportunities) to 'get it right from the start'.

PARENTS AND PROFESSIONALS AS PARTNERS

The majority of service providers for families with children who have learning disabilities now acknowledge the need to encourage active partnership with parents – for the benefit of the family and of the child. Partnership, however, cannot be assumed to be present simply because professionals are working with parents – or because parents wish to be more fully involved in the care of their child. Professionals generally are endeavouring to 'demystify' their work and to be more openly accountable. Integration, as a social as well as an educational policy, recognises that people with severe disabilities will live in the community. Since the majority will continue to live in their own homes, the family must be seen as having a more pro-active relationship with professionals. In a time of scarce resources it has also been suggested that the economics of intervention in the family will be cost-effective, since teaching the parents to pass on new skills will be less time-consuming than working with the child in a separate environment. Additionally, parental involvement in the care and education of *all* children has been more widely supported and it is recognised that 'home' plays a critical role in the development and education of young children. The voluntary sector has additionally emphasised the *right* of parents to be involved and (with the new open access to information provided by the Education Act 1981) it seems probable that many more parents will not only be involved but will actually know the basis for future professional judgments.

The growth of professional willingness to work in partnership with parents must be put in the context of individual family dynamics and the support which is given to parents who may be playing multiple roles. All young children are demanding. Wolkind (1981) has shown the high incidence of depression among young mothers living in inner city areas, where traditional family support may be lacking and where poor housing, lack of services and unemployment may exacerbate the usual problems of rearing young children.

Ann Oakley (1974) noted that 'motherhood has a single long-term goal, which can be described as the mother's own eventual unemployment. A "successful mother" brings up her children to do without her.' Unfortunately the pathways to independence may not be so clear when a child has learning difficulties. Severe disability and lack of practical help may delay the achievement of developmental milestones and provide fewer tangible rewards for hard work and effort. A study by Glendinning (1983) found that 50.1 per cent of severely disabled children over five (361 in the study) could not be left alone for even ten minutes in a day. In these circumstances practical help and involvement in educational programmes must be matched with wider support and recognition of existing family structures. Wilkin (1979) and Baldwin (1985) emphasise the particular burden placed upon mothers, with little support from neighbours or relatives. A factor for consideration in service development must be the special needs of one-parent families.

Cooke and Bradshaw (1986) note that disabled children are more likely than other children to experience at least one spell in a one-parent family. These spells are longer for disabled than non-disabled children and families with a severely disabled child are less likely to be reconstituted. In effect the single parent carer must have special support in order to act as an effective partner and as a relaxed and positive parent of a disabled child.

47

The Honeylands survey (Brimblecombe 1983) shows the importance of not only involving the *whole* family in treatment, counselling and support, but also of the necessity to avoid assuming that stable local communities and extended families will automatically support parents with a disabled child. A report on the Carraigfoyle Paediatric Support Unit in Northern Ireland (Barnardos Irish Division 1984) mirrors these conclusions and notes that 'the importance of family networks was apparent in the course of our work. The extended family often shared in the care of the child and provided emotional support. But sometimes this also brought emotional complications. While giving some emotional support, all parties were under strain as they [the extended family] lacked the necessary information to be able to help adequately.' The Honeylands evaluation similarly found that a 'holistic' approach was impossible without a recognition of the emotional and practical needs of grandparents and siblings. As the Carraigfoyle team concluded after their first two years, 'we learned as the months went by that the unit should be a "family support" unit in the widest possible sense'.

McConachie (1983) has also noted that families may prefer different styles of involvement in the care of a child with learning difficulties – some liking a highly structured approach, others favouring a more 'natural' parental style or finding systematic efforts difficult to sustain.

PARENTS AS EDUCATORS

The increasing popularity of the Portage home teaching scheme for parents of pre-school disabled children has demonstrated the importance of a known, trained and supported home visitor making regular visits to a family in order to monitor the child's progress and to identify goals and structure simple teaching programmes. Portage has been a major source of skill training for professionals as well as for parents. Health visitors, community nurses, home liaison teachers, psychologists and (in some instances) volunteers have learned through using Portage how to work as a team, how to work directly with parents and share skills and expertise and, most importantly, how to offer parents positive action at a time when they may feel depressed and pessimistic about happy outcomes.

Although Portage is primarily offering a home teaching model, it has important lessons for developing flexible team services in a variety of other contexts. It demonstrates the importance of team support for the individual professional and the value of regular contact with families in identifying broader parental needs and alerting services to meet them. Parents also acquire the ability to utilise their knowledge of their child in a meaningful way and to understand the principles behind the practice of any treatment or early intervention programme.

Portage has been successfully modified for use in local authority and NHS residential and day care settings with adolescents and young adults, involving the young people in goal setting and programme plans (Russell 1986). However, the role of the parent as 'educator' is not that of a cheap treatment resource for hard-pressed statutory services. Cunningham and Davis (1985b) note the need to reinforce parental competence; to ensure resources are available and accessible; to provide accurate comprehensible information and to ensure continuity rather than one-off interventions.

THE ROLE OF VOLUNTARY ORGANISATIONS

The contribution of voluntary organisations (whether local groups or national organisations like MENCAP, or self-help groups for 'mixed' disabilities, such as those run by Contact a Family) is still under-used by health, education and social services when helping families with children who have learning disabilities. There is high potential in the voluntary sector for a variety of roles – ranging from befriending and counselling to shared social and leisure activities, practical help and involvement in professional decision making. Many parent groups can not only act as self-advocates in the development of new patterns of care, but can also monitor and evaluate what is already being provided. Shared accountability will mean better services. But it will also entail more mutual respect, honesty and willingness to change. The responsibility for a healthy and positive voluntary sector rests partly on professionals. Referrals to voluntary bodies will increase membership (as well as provide individuals with support). Additionally, the procedures of both the 1981 Education Act and 1986 Disabled Persons Act will necessitate closer liaison between the voluntary and statutory sectors in terms of advocacy and representation. Representation of relevant voluntary organisations in all local planning initiatives will be essential in order to provide not only mutual support but quality control and consumer satisfaction.

RESPITE AND SHORT-TERM CARE

A key factor in family support will be the availability of respite or short-term care. Short-term care developed originally as an emergency service to avert crises and was seen primarily as a means of family relief. A decade ago, the use of such short-term care tended to be in 'block' bookings for the summer or school holidays, but many parents now utilise short-term care on a day basis, with flexibility according to family demands.

The DHSS Social Work Inspectorate Study (1984a) and the evaluation of use of respite services at Honeylands both emphasised the importance of parents being confident that requests for use of respite care would be answered positively. The Honeylands experience was that most families used both planned short-term and emergency care as part of an overall strategy for family support and that effective utilisation of services depended on realistic planning and review of the needs of the whole family.

Both Oswin (1984) and a DHSS social work inspectorate report on family schemes for shared care in Norfolk and Oxfordshire (1984b) identified the importance of recognising that many families will need counselling before their children use any respite care scheme. The DHSS study noted three hurdles for potential users to overcome, namely using any service for the first time, leaving a child overnight and placing a child for a longer period while the parents had a separate holiday. Oswin and the DHSS studies also emphasised the need to build in systematic approaches to evaluating specific schemes in order to ensure that they achieve good quality care.

A key requirement in any respite care scheme must be a clearly defined policy, with guidelines for admission; explicit links with other services for children; parental counselling and participation; flexibility; a neighbourhood basis and – most importantly of all – a recognition of good child care practice in organisation and staff development.

ADOLESCENCE

The majority of family support and intervention services have focused upon the young child with learning difficulties and his or her family. However, recent research (Brimblecombe 1985; Royal College of Physicians 1986) has clearly demonstrated the importance of managing the transition to adult life in a more effective way. The lack of coterminosity in health, education and social services with regard to the age limits of children's services creates considerable problems. Parents may find themselves losing specialist support because it was linked to a school health service provision; respite care because the local authority focuses such services upon children under 18 and general professional guidance at a point when they and their children are facing major challenges and changes. Adolescence can mean a crisis of identity for *all* parents and young people. When the young person has special needs, personal and educational difficulties may be confused by misconceptions about what is 'normal' for all young people and, in particular, by the difficulties many parents experience in accepting adult status for 'children' who may still have areas of dependence and require additional support.

Adolescence also raises the questions of *whose* rights should be paramount, for example the right of the young person to make choices which may go against the aspirations of the parents. Many parents will feel uncertain about accepting their child's ability to participate in informed decision making without positive professional support for some calculated risk taking. In theory the procedures of the 1981 Education Act and 1986 Disabled Persons Act should increase parental expectations – and enable them to share their knowledge and expectations with professionals. In practice many parents are still confused and ambivalent about their new role and lack basic information for understanding the choices open to them. Particular practical problems for parents of young people with special needs in the post-school period will relate to requirements for information on the full range of adult services, with particular reference to opportunities for continuing education; for vocational and prevocational training; for leisure facilities and for continuing assessment and genuine choice about where the young person will wish to live when a move from the family home becomes appropriate (when parents will also require assistance in developing their role in relation to their son or daughter).

Research by Hirst (1983) and Brimblecombe (1985) has indicated the depression, social isolation and lack of self-esteem which can affect both families and their young adult members if inappropriate levels of service are available in the post-school years. At this stage, the needs of the carers and the needs of the young person may appear to diverge and assessment should take careful account of the perceptions, feelings and capabilities of both – with an emphasis on shared decision making and the creation of positive expectations.

COORDINATION OF SERVICES – A TEAM APPROACH

Services for all disabled children have become increasingly multi-professional. The focus upon multi-professional assessment with reference to the 1981 Education Act procedures highlights the often complex shared decision-making processes between different professional agencies and parents in determining the optimum provision for young children who have a variety of special needs. As the Fish committee (Inner London Education Authority 1985) noted, the new generation of parents suffer not so much from the isolation of the 1950s and 60s as from 'overkill', duplication and apparent fragmentation of services.

Problems in professional partnership include:

1 The fact that many professionals and services working with children with learning disabilities and their families will be at different stages of their professional development in terms of expectations for children and families and in their ability to work innovatively as part of multi-professional local services.

2 Although each profession brings expertise and resources, there is some overlap in terms of concerns and roles.

3 The new climate of parental involvement in decision making will mean professionals having to publicly disagree and discuss issues in front of clients. Professionals are (in theory) trained to negotiate. Parents will themselves need training and guidance in order to see negotiation as part of a learning process about their child.

4 Confidentiality (and differing codes of professional conduct) may be barriers to honest discussion and forward planning.

5 Different agencies may have varying priorities for the allocation of their resources.

6 Professionals may themselves take broader or narrower views of their own roles and may need training and support in order to function as an effective team.

7 Since all children with learning disabilities should be seen as part of a broader range of children in the community, many services will need to incorporate more dynamic and child-orientated child care policies in looking at new patterns of service for the children and their families. The principle of integration, as of normalisation, will mean closer liaison with

child care agencies in the community and maximum support of children within integrated local services.

Professionals who are involved with an individual family function in three broad areas. They may provide *treatment*, they may *refer* or they may work *cooperatively*. This latter may cause the greatest difficulty, since it implies accepting the complementary skills of other professional disciplines. Where there are local collaborative structures (such as community mental handicap teams, district handicap teams or child development teams), such partnership may be relatively simple. But the absence of effective teams (or competition within agencies for the management of a particular child) will inhibit parents from utilising services, create professional conflict and minimise partnership with the family.

The development of effective team strategies for meeting the needs of disabled children and their families is still generally inadequate. The DHSS Social Work Inspectorate's report (1984a) found that teams could vary widely in membership and function: 'Many teams were still in their infancy and had yet to prove themselves. Teething troubles seemed less related to internal tensions than to concern about availability of resources for the team.' Conversely, the same report found a wide range of successful team approaches, including a district child handicap management team set up by a health authority but chaired by a divisional social services officer and a multi-disciplinary team for physically handicapped children based on a district handicap team with an assessment playgroup and a range of specialist services. The DHSS report concluded that successful multi-disciplinary teams must have clearly defined roles with particular reference to questions of accountability; their relationships with employing authorities; access to resources and links with specialist and generic facilities. The Honeylands evaluation would also suggest that successful teams must offer mutual support and constantly review policy and practice.

The procedures of formal assessment under section 5 of the 1981 Education Act have been little exploited by health and social services departments as a means of coordinated planning with education authorities, in the best interests of children with disabilities and their families. Formal assessment under the 1981 Act will lead to a 'Statement of special educational needs'. This inter-professional statement (to which parents also contribute and whose professional advice is shared between all participants – including families) in many respects replicates current processes of individual programme planning and could be seen as fore-shadowing the procedures of the Disabled Persons Act which will also require a statement of need, with an indication of how such needs may be met. Since education for children with severe learning difficulties will be concerned with a range of priorities (including the acquisition of independence and social skills), participation in educational decision making by all relevant professional agencies will be essential.

KEY ISSUES IN A COMMUNITY SERVICE FOR FAMILIES WITH A CHILD WHO HAS LEARNING DISABILITIES

1 Assessment, with regular reviews, is essential in monitoring not only a child's development, but also stress levels and changing family circumstances. Such assessment and review should recognise the complementary (but distinct) interests of child and parents within a broad family focus.

2 Parental involvement and effective partnership require constant support and professionals need training in how best to utilise parents' knowledge of their child.

3 Parental reactions to handicaps will vary. Many parents of children with learning disabilities experience their greatest difficulties with traditional 'parental problems' such as feeding, sleeping, behaviour disturbance and childhood illnesses. Key professionals working with families should have a knowledge of *normal* child development and child care, as well as a capacity to cope with specific difficulties relating to the learning disability.

4 A centre or team can act as a base for effective referral of families to neighbourhood community services. Many parents criticise the fragmentation and duplication of services. The team approach avoids such duplication and (with the use of a key worker or named person) ensures that parents are aware of options for help and are able to use them.

5 The focus for all services to families should be the individual programme plan – agreed between parents and professionals, with participation by the child or young person where possible. In the case of children, such programme plans should be seen as action plans and reviewed every six months. The assessment procedures of the 1981 Education Act offer a model for inter-disciplinary assessment and parent participation. Health

authorities and social services departments should ensure that they liaise adequately with their education counterparts to avoid duplication and ensure coordinated services.

6 Parents clearly gain from mutual support and friendship. Health authorities and social services departments should ensure that parents are aware of local self-help and voluntary networks which can offer advice, counselling and practical support. Parent groups and voluntary organisations have an additional role in providing consultative groups for the development of local services and as part of an evaluative process in assessing the effectiveness and appropriateness of current service provision. Some district handicap and community mental handicap teams have members from the voluntary sector; others have clear guidelines for referral and liaison.

7 Many families will need a flexible service, with appropriate patterns of care to cover particular needs. Provision for flexibility necessitates particular attention to patterns of referral and use; to consumer and professional evaluation and to a team approach in order to ensure that families are neither isolated and forgotten nor subject to 'overkill' from competing professionals.

8 Services for children need not only to consider *early* intervention, but to develop a life cycle and incremental approach with particular reference to periods of transition such as transfer to full-time school or to adult services.

9 Definitions of 'family' need should be construed widely, since many children will increasingly live in substitute families or in small group homes in the community. Foster parents or staff acting in *loco parentis* in the community should have access to *parent* services.

10 Since many children with a learning disability will have secondary handicaps and other health problems, it is essential that specialist services ensure that all children have access to good quality primary health care. It is also essential that interprofessional recordkeeping is effective and that issues relating to confidentiality between agencies are resolved at an early stage.

11 Since parents are now legally entitled to have copies of all advice from health, education and social services which is used in producing the 'Statement of special educational

needs' required by the 1981 Education Act, other professional agencies should consider their own protocols with regard to giving parents access to professional information on their child. It should be noted that some health authorities (McFarlane 1986) are now experimenting with parental responsibility for child health record cards and that this shared responsibility appears to greatly increase parental confidence, without alarming or confusing families and without loss of important information.

In conclusion, planning, providing and developing a flexible system of family support following the birth or identification of a disabled child will require imaginative and dynamic approaches between health, education, social services and the voluntary sector. Hilton Davis (Cunningham and Davis 1985b) notes that 'partnership is a relationship in which the professional services work with the parents by making appropriate expertise available to them. The relationship is, therefore, one of complementary expertise, since the expert knowledge of the parents themselves, their aims, their situation, their child complements what the professional can offer'. Good services for children – involving negotiated individual programe plans and agreed collaborative procedures between professionals – will not only maximise the child's development but establish important principles for subsequent services for adults.

Definitional note

In the context of services to children, the use of 'learning disabilities' as the preferred definition to 'mental handicap' may need further clarification. The Education Act 1981 removed the categories of handicap (mental handicap, physical handicap, maladjusted and so on) as established under the Education Act 1944. The Education Act 1981 introduces the concept of 'special educational needs'. Special needs are defined in section 1 (1) as 'a learning difficulty which calls for special educational provision to be made for him (*ie* the child)' and in section 1 (2) 'A child has a learning difficulty if:

(a) he has a significantly greater difficulty in learning than the majority of children of his age: or

(b) he has a disability which either prevents or hinders him from making use of educational facilities of a kind generally provided in schools within the area of the LEA concerned for children of his age: or

(c) he is under the age of five and is, or would be if special educational provision were not made for him, likely to fall within paragraph (a) or (b) when over that age.'

Learning difficulties (often informally called 'learning disabilities') in the formal assessment procedures of the 1981 Act may include sensory, social and physical disabilities unrelated to 'learning disabilities' as used in this book.

In the context of local assessment procedures and collaborative planning, education authorities now use the broad definitions of the 1981 Act and avoid the old labels but different terminologies may be used by social services departments and health professionals, making it essential that mutual understanding is reached on the status of individual children. It is also essential that the implications for families of imprecise or poorly expressed definitions are appreciated. Notwithstanding these difficulties, the growing ability of children's services to express needs in broad terms which avoid premature labelling but permit signposting to appropriate resources merits wider consideration by agencies working with adults with learning disabilities.

References

Baldwin S (1985) The costs of caring. London, Routledge and Kegan Paul.

Barnardos (1984) Carraigfoyle paediatric support unit: the first two years. Belfast, Barnardos Irish Division.

Bicknell J (1981) Right from the start. London, Royal Society for Mentally Handicapped Children and Adults.

Brimblecombe F S W (1983) Honeylands progress report. Exeter, Paediatric Research Unit, Royal Devon and Exeter Hospital.

Brimblecombe F S W (1985) The needs of handicapped young adults. Department of Child Health, University of Exeter.

Cooke K and Bradshaw J (1986) Child disablement, family dissolution and reconstitution. Developmental Medicine and Child Neurology 28: 610–16.

Cunningham C and Davis H (1985a) Early parent counselling. In: Craft M, Bicknell J and Hollins S (eds). Mental handicap: a multidisciplinary approach. London, Ballière Tindall.

Cunningham C and Davis H (1985b) Working with parents: frameworks for collaboration. Milton Keynes, Open University Press.

DHSS Social Work Inspectorate (1984a) Services for handicapped children: schemes and development in England. London, DHSS.

DHSS Social Work Inspectorate, Banks S, Grizzell R (1984b) A study of family placement schemes for the shared care of handicapped children in Norfolk and Oxfordshire. London, DHSS.

Glendinning C (1983) Unshared care – parents and their disabled children. London, Routledge and Kegan Paul.

Hewett S (1970) Handicapped children and their families: a survey. Nottingham, Nottingham University Child Development Research Unit.

Hirst M (1983) Young people with disabilities: what happens after 16? Child Care, Health and Development 9: 273–84.

Inner London Education Authority (1985) Educational opportunities for all? The report of the committee reviewing provision to meet special education needs (Chairman Mr John Fish). London, ILEA.

McConachie H (1983) Fathers, mothers, siblings: how do they see themselves? In: Mittler P and McConachie H (eds). Parents, professionals and mentally handicapped people: approaches to partnership. London, Croom Helm.

MacFarlane A (1986) Parents' rights and children's rights. Concern 58, Spring 1986: 6–7.

Oakley A (1974) The sociology of housework. London, Martin Robinson.

Oswin M (1984) They keep going away. London, King Edward's Hospital Fund for London.

Parliament (1976) Fit for the future: report of the Committee on Child Health Services (Chairman Professor S D M Court). Cmnd 6684. London, HMSO.

Parliament (1978) Special educational needs: report of the Committee of Enquiry into the Education of Handicapped Children and Young People (Chairman Mrs H M Warnock). Cmnd 7212. London, HMSO.

Royal College of Physicians (1986) The young disabled adult. London, RCP.

Russell P (1986) Portage – pre-schoolers, parents and professionals. In: Cameron R J (ed). Portage: ten years of achievement. London, NFER/Nelson.

Wilkin D (1979) Caring for the mentally handicapped child. London, Croom Helm.

Wolkind S (1981) Depression in mothers of young children. Archives of Diseases in Childhood 56, 1: 1–13.

Ritchard Brazil and Nan Carle

An ordinary home life

In this chapter we explore the kinds of experiences which should be offered to people with a learning disability in a housing or home environment. We also describe two organisations trying to realise these aspirations while retaining their ability to meet planned objectives for service provision. We accept, however, that major challenges still exist to an ordinary home life. We focus on some of these using the sorts of questions that people with learning disabilities themselves are asking about our services.

It appears that in many areas there is a contrast between the principles that were set out in *An Ordinary Life* (King's Fund 1980) and the types of services that are being developed. We argue that the next stage towards an ordinary home life will be to consider more actively the *empowerment* of users.

Both of the organisations that we describe have attempted to address this issue. We can conclude from their efforts that extending the practice of multi-agency collaboration for planning and management purposes provides a useful framework in which to test our ability to share control over services with our users.

WHY IS AN ORDINARY HOME LIFE SO IMPORTANT?

Most of us take our homes for granted. They are central to our way of life and serve as the fulcrum around which all else turns. A home means something different to each of us and enhances our lives in many different ways. Here are a few common themes.

It's a supportive place to go out from.
It's a nice place to be.
It's a place where you can be alone.
It's a place you don't get turned out from.
It's a place to unwind.
It's a place where you can do what you like.
It's a place where you choose who else lives there, who comes to visit and for how long.
It's a place that expresses who you are.

Individuals may view these descriptions differently, but there can be no doubt that most of us would fight to preserve a nice supportive place where we have control. We would fight to protect our identities and our right to have the kind of home we want.

Unfortunately, people with learning disabilities don't very often have the tools with which to fight for a good home life. This is more evident in services where decisions affecting them are made by others who are often strangers to them. These circumstances can lead to some of the following experiences.

Leaving the family home and neighbourhood to live in a strange place.

Being part of a group of people labelled as having 'learning disabilities' or 'mental handicap'.

Lacking control over who else lives and works in the house.

Having little tenure or security.

Having few possessions other than small items such as radios, TVs and perhaps some furniture.

Being seen as someone who is 'taking' rather than 'giving' or contributing to the life of the neighbourhood.

People with learning disabilities, therefore, need to be given the tools with which to secure and preserve an ordinary home life. Because the levels and types of support needed will vary, service providers should constantly redefine their aims bearing in mind that resources are precious. Regardless of the severity of an individual's disability, provision of the following could be regarded as desirable goals:

– security of tenure
– ownership of possessions and property
– control over where and with whom they live
– the ability to sustain old relationships and create new ones outside the service world
– clear information on who will be doing what and when on their behalf
– support that is intensive and relevant to their personal needs
– being treated as a neighbour and valued member of the community at large

Since these are ideal accomplishments, levels of success will vary, but the experience and knowledge gained with each success increase our ability to enable people with learning disabilities to become valued members of a community.

TWO ORGANISATIONS IN PRACTICE

The Camden experience

Coral used to cook in hospital. Often, when the staff were under pressure and 16 meals had to be produced in the ward's own little kitchen at supper time, Coral would offer to help. After a time the staff relied on her. It took a long time to prepare plates of sausage and egg and usually when she had finished cooking the last serving for others, she would sit down to eat her own meal by herself. The others had finished.

Coral now lives in a house in Camden with three others. She enjoys cooking and takes responsibility for many of the meals that she and her friends eat. She is beginning to experiment, extending her repertoire and testing new products that she buys at the local shop. When she cooks for the others in the house they generally eat their meals together. Nobody likes cleaning up afterwards.

Nick's family came from Cyprus when he was small. Nick sometimes gets confused and calls the hospital he was in 'prison'. Nick likes to run and goes to work in the bakery very early every morning. He likes the emptiness of the streets and his job suits him because the other staff in the bakery start early as well. He gets home most days before three o'clock and usually sleeps until supper time. The support workers who spend time in the house with Nick and the other people who live there, are often at home when he gets up. Nick likes company in the evening.

When the housing committee at CSMH (Camden Society for People with a Mental Handicap) meets, the meetings themselves rarely last more than two hours. Most people get bored if it takes longer than this. They come regularly, however, because they know that important decisions often get made which affect their lives. They have learnt that the staff and volunteers who also come to the meetings don't enjoy them much either. Everybody joins in and the Chair works very hard to make sure anyone who wants to speak can have the chance. Before the people with learning disabilities started coming, the meetings took a lot longer. Nobody thinks they achieved more, though.

These illustrations are taken from the comprehensive service for people with learning disabilities that is being developed in the London Borough of Camden. Currently, over 40 people live in a variety of housing situations supported by a network of peripatetic staff. The service began in 1976, and over the years has expanded as more people leave institutional care and return to live in the area. The ultimate aim is to provide a comprehensive service in Camden for anyone with any level of disability.

The Camden service, which is run jointly by users, CSMH, Camden Social Services and Bloomsbury Health Authority, provides a variety of supported housing dispersed throughout the borough. People live alone or in small groups with other individuals of their choice. Decisions about vacancies are made by the people who live in the house concerned. The service's role here is to introduce people who might fill a vacancy and ease the transition of a successful candidate.

Other decisions relating to the housing service as a whole are made by the housing committee of CSMH. People with a learning disability influence the level of rents, use of move-on accommodation, development of new properties and numerous details about general management and maintenance issues. The service also houses non-disabled people who hold licences on exactly the same basis as the other service users. Non-disabled residents have no explicit role other than a general contribution to the shared housing environment.

Staff play a supporting and enabling role. Like other services in Lewisham and Southwark, Bristol (Wells Road) and South Wales (NIMROD), staff in Camden participate in a process in which the goal involved is not care or protection, but rather enabling users of the service to benefit from enhanced community presence, wider relationships, extended choice, growing individual competence and greater respect from others (O'Brien 1987).

Over time, the Camden staff have come to see their input as a combination of experience and expertise together with the desire to help people with learning disabilities face new challenges. Staff are regarded as resources whose primary function is to contribute to a learning process which will enhance the experience of living at home in the community. Staff are not attached to particular houses, but to individuals, and this relationship is the focus of their work.

User participation in management is a major goal of this service. This means that staff teams act as the link between promotion and development of the service's policies and their impact on users. They work alongside people with disabilities to implement policies and report on their effects. In contrast to much established practice, they are, in effect, advocates on behalf of the service.

The service in Camden is not perfect and would not claim to be so. Although problems exist, there is general agreement about its objectives among users, professionals and volunteers. The housing service forms part of an expanding network of employment, education, recreation and advocacy services which are linked and strengthened by a common purpose.

During its first ten years, the Camden service grew incrementally as the cooperation and collaboration of the participants matured. If there is tension between the parties involved, then it can be perceived as largely positive. New challenges are constantly being identified and strategies devised to meet them.

The Southwark Consortium

Reaching the stage where agencies are able to address real service issues rather than merely performing the ritual dance of professional collaboration remains a major challenge. Our vision of an 'ordinary home life' is becoming widely shared. Its targets are clear: to provide a flexible range of housing and support options to meet individual needs in ways which are designed to help people live as full a life as possible (Towell 1985). However, many service agencies have still to learn the language of mutual collaboration, especially when a new comprehensive network is being established as part of the closure of an institution and existing local services are minimal. Such a situation has begun to be successfully addressed in Southwark.

Southwark, like many local authority areas, does not have coterminous boundaries with the health authorities that operate in its area – Lewisham and North Southwark and Camberwell. Together, however, these statutory agencies are faced with the responsibility of providing comprehensive services for people with learning disabilities leaving Darenth Park Hospital as well as those already living in the community.

In 1984 the statutory agencies, local voluntary organisations, three housing associations and the Southwark Adult Education Institute combined to form the Southwark Consortium. Its primary purpose was to provide an effective collaborative forum which would enable the implementation of agreed plans to develop services for people in the borough. It is worth pointing out that the consortium did not and still does not see its role as a planning body. It is accepted that each organisation involved has its own set of objectives. The consortium tries to ensure that these dovetail together and, most importantly, that issues relating to the style, content and delivery of services continue to be addressed.

There is a tendency for agencies to become so involved in service delivery that they lose sight of the individual client. The Southwark Consortium tries to redress the balance. Staff employed by the consortium, who have responsibility for development, finance, housing management and support issues, consistently advise, link and coordinate the activities of service providing agencies. The overall aim is to provide one Southwark service which is run in partnership by all concerned.

Admittedly, however, the consortium still remains fundamentally flawed since service users have not been full participants in the management of the service. Failure to properly involve users in the service is often inherited from previous service design decisions. From the point of view of the service providers, one of the most powerful aspects of an ordinary home life is the chance it offers to meet service goals – drawn out of larger plans – which strive towards an ideal of community care. As a result, services often group people together in houses because of their disability as the most effective way of delivering support in a coordinated and reasonably efficient manner. Staff do not refer to people's property; rather, they talk about their 'project'. The consortium, therefore, like many newly developing services, is still far from being accountable to users. This is because designing an accountable service is not often a major component of service planning.

The constraints that exist in trying to bring services closer to users are beginning to be addressed by the consortium. Its initial purpose centred around the need to collaborate effectively, since no single agency is in a position to deliver a true multi-disciplinary service. This view is now extending to the involvement of users. The Southwark service, provided by a range of agencies, cannot be homogeneous. No one organisation dominates the philosophy or practice of the service or the form that the service will take. As a result there is room to consider the wider issues of accountability and control from the perspective of organisations with similar goals working together. The consortium acts as the forum in which challenges to the direction and content of organisations' policies can be addressed.

Inside the organisations themselves, issues of control and ownership of the service are too easily subjugated by the contingencies of finance, planning and management. In the open forum of the consortium the organisations involved are more able to cope with the challenge of accountability, free of internal service constraints.

If the movement towards strengthening the voice of consumers is to have real impact, then consumers, like the organisations that provide the service, must have an open and accessible forum in which to air their concerns. The consortium provides a meeting place where the consumer's views will be given more priority than they often are at health authority or social services committee meetings.

The Camden service has been gradually extended over ten years. It retains a true sense of its objectives on behalf of and together with its clients. The Southwark Consortium has attempted to create a tradition and consensus over a very short period. It is now ready to redress the balance and make sure that the future blends individual self-determination with organisational coherence.

QUESTIONS WHICH SERVICE USERS ARE ASKING US

Although we have begun to clear new paths, there are still many challenges facing us on our journey to enable people with learning disabilities to live an ordinary home life. Some of the questions they might be asking us are as follows.

Who will I live with and where?

How we enable people to choose who they live with is a challenge we stumble around. Organisations have their own goals which very often conflict with what an individual wants or needs. The smaller the setting, the more personalised the support can be. An ordinary house lessens the distance and increases respect between the person with the label and local people not labelled. It also offers more opportunity for exploration in and around the neighbourhood since it provides a stable base. Questions are beginning to be formulated about how we can create conditions whereby people may choose where they live and with whom.

What help will I get?

Small houses offer the greatest challenge and risk to service providers. It is difficult to manage and support staff and monitor the quality of the service in disparate houses. Who knows what really goes on there? What sort of training do staff need in order to help people to make informed choices? Staff and their clients will be in very close proximity. How do we help them to cope with the paid/unpaid, equal/unequal aspects of such situations?

Why do I have to live with other people with learning disabilities? I don't even know them!

For service providers this will remain a challenge for a very long time. A great deal has been done so that people live in smaller groups with a more natural and personalised home life. However, we are still very much in danger of transplanting smaller wards into ordinary houses linked by staff groups on bicycles and in cars. We still have to tackle how to enable people to maintain, and in some instances rebuild, links with their family and friends outside the world of learning disability. This is made particularly difficult when houses where labelled people live are all in the same part of town (by accident?).

Can I live in an ordinary house even if my behaviour really challenges us both? Will you make me leave?

People who have lived in institutions for many years and have exhibited challenging behaviour do not divest themselves of that behaviour merely by moving into a small local house in the community. It may be just another move which disturbs the continuity or intensity of the service being received. A new environment requires support which is highly motivated. Very often a better environment facilitates improved behaviour, but it certainly isn't everything or people wouldn't have been sent off to institutions in the first place. The move from one place to another is likely to be very unsettling especially for people who don't like changes in their lives.

How can I live an ordinary home life when the house is full of staff?

The challenge here is one of ensuring that the service is consistent and does not discourage others from becoming involved. Too much activity around a house can either make people feel that 'others are doing it, I don't need to', or 'I wonder what in the world goes on in there?' or 'I miss my parking space. Why should I always be put out?' The role of staff in a neighbourhood of which they are not a part is a new challenge.

CONCLUSION

The path from saying where we want to go, to getting there, is probably longer than we thought. In the last few years it has been shown that services can develop substantially without sacrificing the goals for individuals set out in *An Ordinary Life*.

Tension exists between the pressure to develop services and our requirement that they should all be of the highest standards. This chapter has tried to address some of these tensions and suggest ways of dealing with them.

The next area of work will be to enable people to live with whomever they please in houses they rent or own themselves. The constant challenge is to increase service to those who need it while decreasing the amount of control service providers have over their lives.

Unfortunately, organisations often have lives of their own which can become separated from the goals they are trying to achieve. The collaborative services described in this chapter are cited as two examples, certainly not perfect, of how organisations working together with a common commitment and a shared vision can retain their direction and perspective. In both cases sharing control with service users is achievable. Our task is to create the conditions that make it possible. The long-term impact of our service needs to be evaluated against our ability to provide and run services together and with our users. In an ordinary home life the provision of an appropriate house for a person to live in is only the first step. The approaches in Camden and Southwark offer a vehicle for further testing and developing of ideas about services in a creative and positive manner. Opportunities are being explored by the service agencies through a collaborative framework which is far removed from the day-to-day problems of the service bureaucracy.

References

King's Fund (1980) An ordinary life: comprehensive locally-based residential services for mentally handicapped people (project paper 24). London, King Edward's Hospital Fund for London.
O'Brien J (1987) A guide to personal futures planning. In: Bellamy G T and Wilcox B (eds). A comprehensive guide to the activities catalog: an alternative curriculum for youth and adults with severe disabilities. Baltimore, Paul H Brookes.
Towell D (1985) Residential needs and services. In: Craft M, Bicknell J and Hollins S (eds). Mental handicap – a multi-disciplinary approach. London, Ballière Tindall.

Linda Ward

Developing opportunities
for an ordinary community life

This chapter explores what is involved in enabling individuals with learning disabilities to enjoy a fuller, better quality of life in the community. It looks in turn at three related questions. What is meant by an ordinary community life? What kind of approach is needed by services in this area? What difference does access to a fuller community life make to the quality of people's lives?

'AN ORDINARY COMMUNITY LIFE' – WHAT DOES IT MEAN?

Since the publication of *An Ordinary Life* in 1980, the fundamental importance of ordinary domestic housing as a starting point for the pursuit of 'ordinary lives' by people with learning disabilities has become clear.

More recently, people have also become aware of the equal importance of good daytime opportunities for residents of these 'ordinary' homes. Nationally, this concern has been reflected in King's Fund publications like *An Ordinary Working Life* and *The Employment of People with Mental Handicap* (see Appendix I), the Independent Development Council's *Living Like Other People* (1985) and some innovative ventures in this field, discussed in the next chapter.

We have now come to realise that even good daytime opportunities and high quality residential services are not enough. People with learning disabilities – like any other people – want more from life than that. They too want to 'belong' in their neighbourhood, pursue enjoyable activities in their spare time, use local shops and leisure facilities, join local groups and residents' associations, and have the chance to develop relationships and friendships with other people in their area. Concern has shifted to appropriate steps and strategies for offering them a chance to become a valued part of their neighbourhood – the chance, if you like, of 'an ordinary community life'.

Thinking of how to enable people to gain access to a fuller life in the community raises some fundamental issues. There is concern about the involvement of service providers in this area and the danger of trying to design or routinely *prescribe* something called 'an ordinary community life' for everyone who has a learning disability. The risk here is of causing unwanted side effects: creating very specialised, unordinary, blanket services for people with learning disabilities which result in *segregation*, not *integration*, and which may destroy or supplant informal networks already existing in the neighbourhood.

There is, however, an alternative, more appropriate, way in which services can promote access to a fuller, better life in the community. This is by fostering and supporting a variety of opportunities for integration: the use of local facilities like shops, post offices; pubs and cafés; involvement in neighbourhood networks of different kinds (at a formal level, community associations and informally, reciprocal arrangements with neighbours over keeping spare keys, feeding pets, looking out for people's property while they are away on holiday and so on); and participation in local leisure activities. All of this helps to develop the relationships which for many of us are the key to a good quality of life.

The idea is not, of course, that services should try to create all these kinds of opportunities themselves. Their most important role may be to bolster existing informal networks alongside a variety of other agencies, resources and people, both professional and non-professional. An example of how one service has approached this role in practice is given later.

In order to create opportunities for 'an ordinary community life' we need to have some idea of what we're trying to achieve. What do we mean by 'community' or 'social' life? What do we mean by 'ordinary'?

Different people will have different ideas, according to their own circumstances and experiences. Whether we're men or women, in work or unemployed, have children or not, live with a partner or on our own, and our different ethnic backgrounds all influence what we want or expect from our social or community life. What we get depends on many factors – whether we live in an urban or rural area, near or far from our families; whether we have jobs and can pay for some of the key ingredients of a fuller life – phone calls, car or bus trips, discos, concerts, membership fees, admission tickets, sports equipment and so on.

Clearly, an 'ordinary community life' will mean slightly different things to different people. Broadly speaking, though, we are talking about developing opportunities for people to become valued members of their communities and to enjoy a fuller, better quality of life according to their own individual circumstances and desires.

SOME IDEAS

When 50 people in Somerset talked to Dorothy Atkinson about their lives in the community after leaving a mental handicap hospital they spoke largely of the different kinds of *social relationships* they had: with family, in their households, at work, with neighbours and friends. On the whole, those with more relationships rated themselves happier than those with fewer.

> Not surprisingly, individuals vary in how they rate the quality of their lives. At one extreme, Edgar describes himself as 'very, very happy'; at the other extreme, Geoffrey describes himself as 'very, very lonely'. Their lives, and lifestyles, are indeed very different. Edgar has regular and positive contact with his family, he shares house with two congenial companions, he has a job which brings him into contact with workmates, and he has made friends in the neighbourhood. Geoffrey, on the other hand, has lost all contact with his family. He lives alone. He has no job. He has no friends, and he is on bad terms with his neighbours. (Atkinson and Ward 1987)

In this study of the range and variety of lifestyles and social relationships, some key points stood out. First, the importance of a *companion* (whether family member, fellow householder or friend) in enabling people to venture out and sample new experiences which may in turn lead to new relationships based on shared interests. Those living in a shared home, with easy access to a companion, may be at an advantage here. Second, the significance of a *job* (or other daytime activity such as volunteer helper, club member or homemaker) as a source of potential social contacts. Third, the value of *reciprocity* in relationships, so that individuals become part of a network of 'giving' (shopping, gardening or other household chores for elderly relatives or neighbours, for example) as well as 'receiving'.

Although many of the people in Dorothy Atkinson's study were relatively happy, only five of the fifty had moved on from acceptance in the community to becoming an active participant in the web of neighbourhood relationships. All five had done so by contributing to the well-being of other people or developing relationships which were reciprocal. Ralph and Enid, for example, a married couple, helped elderly and handicapped people in their neighbourhood. Between them they had spent 47 years in long-stay hospitals as recipients of services. Now the roles were reversed. As voluntary helpers in their neighbourhood they had a purpose and a sense of belonging. This was also true of three other people in the study who shared a house together.

> Edgar, Robert and Norman participate in local events, and frequent local places. They enter the carnival, drink in the pub, and invite neighbours and friends to birthday parties, and in for Christmas drinks. They do football pools with neighbours, an activity which involves reciprocal house calls. ... They are part of their neighbourhood, they are on first name terms with people in their street and nearby streets, and with people they meet in the pub. They have developed reciprocal relationships not only with Pauline, but with John, Daphne, Dave, Pete and others. (Atkinson and Ward 1987)

Most people in the study, however, had settled for far less than this. Although some spoke proudly of new relationships formed and old ones kept, others described loneliness and their disappointment at not having extended their social network.*

Service planners and providers have been slow to realise that settling into an ordinary neighbourhood does not automatically ensure community integration or a high quality of life. The following section outlines some practical strategies adopted by one community service to try to address these issues.

'AN ORDINARY COMMUNITY LIFE' – WHAT KIND OF SERVICE STRATEGY IS REQUIRED?

In many areas, service planners and providers have in the past chosen to adopt a broadly non-interventionist approach with regard to the development of residents' social or community lives, in the belief or hope that integration into the local community will gradually happen of its own accord (Atkinson and Ward 1986). On the positive side, this has meant a welcome absence of 'interference' or 'prescription' by local services. On the negative side, however, two risks have become clear: people may fail to form relationships and become socially isolated; alternatively, they may develop social relationships exclusively within the 'handicapped' world, and never become integrated in the wider community at all.

To avoid these outcomes, some local services have now begun to adopt a more interventionist approach. Staff, in conjunction with

71

families, friends, volunteers and, of course, the individuals themselves, have put time, thought and energy into rebuilding original family relationships, sustaining relationships in new homes and making friends and acquaintances at work, through other daytime activities and in the neighbourhood. Individuals moving from hospital into new homes in the community are helped to renew former relationships with friends, relatives, neighbours, acquaintances and members of staff. When people have moved back into the neighbourhood where they grew up, old contacts have been remembered and rediscovered, as memories are jogged and half-remembered leads followed up. Sometimes relatives and acquaintances reappear and become an active part of the individual's life. New relationships have also been established as individuals, accompanied by a friend, relative or helper, have gone to local pubs, clubs, evening classes and so on. Ideas, examples and experiences in all these areas are described elsewhere (Atkinson and Ward 1986, 1987).

The Wells Road Service in South Bristol adopted this kind of interventionist approach. This patch-based, small-scale local service (catchment area three square miles; population 35,000) was established in 1982 by the Bristol and Weston Health Authority. It had two interlinked components. The *residential service*, staffed by residential support workers and their manager(s), was to provide a network of different kinds of homes, with appropriate support, using ordinary domestic housing along the lines suggested in *An Ordinary Life*. The *community support service*, staffed by two community support workers, was to offer support and opportunities to other adults in the area, particularly those still living at home with their families.

Both parts of the service placed a high priority on developing opportunities for individuals to enjoy a wide range of new experiences and social relationships. The community support service was unusual, however, in its focus on adults living in the family home. Many community services confine their attention to individuals recently discharged from mental handicap hospitals while neglecting those who have lived in the community all their lives.

Another unusual feature of the community support service was its overt commitment to improving the quality of life available to its clients by developing individually tailored opportunities for integration as outlined earlier. The goal was to achieve something more than the bare minimum of crisis intervention work offered by many overstretched community services.

The innovative nature of the community support workers' brief was enhanced by their appointment on unorthodox (for the NHS) administrative and clerical scales. This was to permit the recruitment of staff with a variety of backgrounds, qualifications and experience relevant to these new posts, rather than restricting recruitment to a single occupational or professional group. The hope was that community staff would respond to people's needs and wishes flexibly and with creativity. They would develop (in conjunction with local people, professionals and agencies) new options and opportunities which were right for particular individuals, rather than offering standard service responses derived from a particular professional background, approach or training.

The two community staff appointed in early 1983 (on the general administrative assistant grade of the administrative and clerical scale) had backgrounds in education and adult training centres respectively. (Information about the selection criteria employed and details of their induction programme and job description are given in Ward 1984.) The two original community staff were joined in 1984 by a part-time colleague who knew the local area and had a background in residential, home aide and voluntary work.

The role of the community support staff evolved over the years. In cooperation with other key people – family, friends, neighbours, local voluntary and community groups and other professionals – they tried to create new opportunities for individuals with learning disabilities in the area. As their knowledge of individuals grew, so did the experience and expertise needed to develop initiatives tailored to those individuals. The preferences and needs which emerged at individual programme plan meetings were very significant here. For example, a variety of educational opportunities were developed – a small special weekly class at a community centre, a special (segregated) evening class at a local college and eventually the integration of a number of individuals into a variety of ordinary mainstream evening classes of their own choice. While maintaining existing networks of support for individuals and their families, staff extended opportunities to participate in local leisure activities, make new friends, and, in a few cases, gain work experience or permanent employment. (More information about the role and activities of the community staff is given in Ward 1986, 1987.)

A key question is to what extent this innovative approach succeeded. Some of its successes are obvious, particularly the initiatives in housing, leisure and adult education (described in

Ward 1986). The less obvious successes implicit in the fuller lives of some individuals which ensued – are described later.

Establishing and maintaining an innovative service of this kind is not trouble-free. There has been some resistance to the idea that those already living in the community should receive more than the usual crisis intervention service. There is also some feeling that efforts to develop new opportunities and relationships within the community are 'frills' in comparison with the more immediate pressures to settle those just moving out of hospital. Whether service planners or providers subscribing to this viewpoint would regard the same areas of their own lives as 'frills' is a different question.

For reasons explored more fully elsewhere (Ward 1987) the community support workers in Bristol are now to be phased out. The stories that follow bear their own testimony, however, to the significant impact that one community support service has had on the quality of some individuals' lives.

'AN ORDINARY COMMUNITY LIFE' – WHAT DIFFERENCE DOES IT MAKE?

The pen-pictures that follow are brief accounts of the impact of the Wells Road community support service on the lives of four local residents – Martin Hill, Susan Johnson, Tom Bryant and David Wilson (not their real names).

Martin Hill

By nature, Martin Hill is quite a shy young man. He used to spend all his spare time at home. Since he met Bridget Freeman, a community support worker with the Wells Road service, things have changed. Now Martin has at least two regular nights out every week. He started off going to a special evening class for people with learning disabilities, organised by Bridget and her colleague, Janice Cotterell, at the local technical college. Once he'd got some confidence there, he decided he'd like to move on to an ordinary evening class in music. He now meets with a group of friends every Tuesday to make music together, with Martin playing guitar and recorder. He's been involved in a couple of concerts, and enjoys the parties that the group organises from time to time. Martin has also discovered he enjoys cooking. He's moved on quickly, with Bridget's help, from learning to make a cup of tea, to cooking a simple meal at home. Now he's joined an evening cookery class to extend his range a bit.

All in all, Martin's life is very different now from how it looked when he left school a few years ago. Although he's always enjoyed music, any idea of playing in a concert would have seemed out of the question then. He'd always been interested in transport but when he first met Bridget his parents still accompanied him to the bus stop every morning to get the bus across town to the sheltered workshop where he works. Now Martin travels all over Bristol by bus on his own. He's acquired a collection of timetables for all the local services and helps family and friends plan their journeys. He says he'd like to learn to drive a car, but neither he nor his family could afford it.

Martin had some help with getting involved in his new activities through the Wells Road Service. It's mainly been a question of building up his confidence, providing opportunities and encouragement. His family have needed assurance too that he can cope safely with greater independence. They now take great pride in his achievements. They've noticed the changes in him. He goes to concerts and discos, which he wouldn't do before. As Mrs Hill comments, 'He likes the fashionable clothes now. He won't wear just anything. He likes to be with the times. He's become much more sociable and self-confident too. He talks more to people now ... He wouldn't take to nobody before.' Comparing Martin's first individual programme plan, where he set himself the tasks of learning to make a cup of tea and tie his shoelaces, and his current plans to enrol in a music workshop and organise a coach trip for himself and a friend, it's clear that Martin's life has opened up a lot.

Susan Johnson

It wasn't long ago that Susan Johnson spent every afternoon having a nap. Her tablets made her very drowsy, and there wasn't a lot to do anyway. Since she and her mother met Bridget Freeman, there's a bit more to look forward to – to begin with, a small weekly class with other people with learning disabilities, now a weekly keep-fit class at the local community centre and literacy and social skills sessions at her home.

Evenings have livened up a bit too after Susan, with Bridget's help, joined a social club which meets weekly. There's also the possibility of a holiday this summer, which would be the first for many years. With the support of their GP, Mrs Johnson has managed to reduce Susan's drugs recently, which has helped Susan concentrate and enjoy life a bit more. There's also been some help on how to diet so that Susan can maybe lose a little weight.

Susan and her mother lead a quiet and sheltered life, and until recently Susan (now in her early 40s) rarely went out at all. She still gets anxious outside a very sheltered setting, and people at Wells Road have had to learn that it's difficult for Susan to cope with a lot of new things at once. There's a much better balance now.

Neither Susan nor her mother expected that the sorts of activities she now enjoys would be possible. Now they are interested in planning other new things. Mrs Johnson is positive about the changes that have taken place since they've had contact with the Wells Road Service, and says of the community staff: 'They're learning her things, aren't they? These other ladies and gents [past social workers] more or less came to talk to *me* to see how *I* was getting on. Now *she's* drawn into everything, she's not left out of anything, she's one of us, if you like. ... She talks more – her sentences are not just "yes", "no", now. It's full sentences because we're all talking to her more, and she's mixing more ... Oh, she is getting on. They've done quite a bit for her. They've brought her out, if you know what I mean.'

What else does Mrs Johnson think that Susan has got from the Wells Road Service? 'Company and friendship and that. People being interested in her.'

Tom Bryant

Tom Bryant looks back over the last couple of years with some satisfaction and a real sense of achievement. Once seen as the 'least able' member of his family, he's now the only one in work. He's proud of holding down a job and no longer needing 'looking after'. After many years in an institution for people with learning disabilities, his sense of self-esteem, and of having 'done it all himself' is very strong.

Things were very different, and difficult, until recently. Other people in his family have special problems too, which has led to some local hostility on the estate where they live. It's also meant that in the past Tom's potential, and problems, have sometimes been prejudged by some professionals to whom the family is well known.

Meeting people from the Wells Road Service has helped to break this vicious circle. For Tom, like Martin, it's been mainly a question of building up confidence through new opportunities and providing educational and work experiences, and the associated help he's needed to benefit from these (learning to get around by bus, buying some new clothes and so on).

Tom will need some help in different areas of his life for quite some time yet, alongside continuing health care to regulate his epilepsy, which is a big handicap for him at the moment. Holding down a job on the local community programme has been a huge step forward, however. 'A year ago I never thought I could do any of this,' he says.

David Wilson

For David Wilson the past two or three years have brought some unexpected changes to his sheltered and orderly life at home with his loving parents. A quiet, retiring man, without employment, he spent his days in his room with books, records, and the radio. Lots of family members and neighbours looked in, but he rarely stepped outside his front door.

The family's association with the Wells Road Service has helped David with the changes that have taken place since then. At 38, he's making up for some lost time and opportunities.

. Kathleen Morgan and her husband Ted have played a key role in opening up David's life in innumerable ways. Recruited as a volunteer by the Wells Road Service, Kathleen has become a close friend and advocate, trusted by David and his family alike. Through Kathleen and Ted, David's horizons have widened enormously. He's participated in a whole new range of experiences and activities with them outside of his family home.

Through Janice Cotterell, his community support worker, he's had access to new opportunities for learning too, in a small weekly group for a few people with learning disabilities meeting at a local community centre, and later, weekly literacy sessions at home. Through that group he's got to know Sarah Hardy and her family, who are now special friends. He and Sarah, with Janice and Bridget, have enjoyed all kinds of new experiences together, including day trips and a first ever night away from home. More recently, David's joined a weekly keep-fit class and he's started learning to swim at the local pool.

Most significantly of all, David's coped with leaving home and settling in with two other men in a well-supported home close by. Sadly, the move was precipitated by his mother's death, which brought forward the careful plans which had already been made for a move in the near future. Kathleen has been a key figure for

David in this difficult time. She broke the news to him about his mother's death and, along with Wells Road staff and the rest of his family, helped him in his grieving. In the past, David's parents were sometimes anxious about how David would manage without them. Now his family are happy to see how well he's managed to adjust to, and enjoy, his new life and his new home.

CONCLUSION

For Martin Hill, Susan Johnson, Tom Bryant and David Wilson (and for many other individuals in the Wells Road area) one key to a fuller life has been a local community support service. In a few other parts of Britain, for example South Glamorgan, similar services perform a similar role (Humphreys *et al* 1986). Elsewhere, ordinary people are becoming involved in the lives of individuals with learning disabilities as neighbours, fellow students, advocates and simply friends, and it is through these personal relationships and shared activities that the idea of 'an ordinary community life' is becoming real. At the King's Fund Centre, a subgroup of the original 'an ordinary life' working party is meeting to produce a follow-up publication on the theme of 'an ordinary community life'.

From the experience of these individuals and services, and from our own personal experience, it is clear how significant friendships, relationships and opportunities for participation in the local community are for the quality of people's lives. The need for enormous sensitivity and awareness on the part of service planners and providers is also clear – not only in appreciating the fundamental importance of these aspects of our lives, but also in recognising that needs and desires will vary from person to person according to gender, age, colour, culture, class, religion, family, personal circumstances and so on.

At the moment, no one has the 'last word' on how best to offer people with learning disabilities a fuller, better quality of life in the community. Only the 'first words' are clear – that opportunities for participation in the community, friendships, relationships, reciprocity and feeling a valued part of the neighbourhood are important to all of us. If we are serious about our attempts to work towards 'an ordinary life' these are issues we cannot afford to ignore.

Acknowledgments

Thanks are due to the Joseph Rowntree Memorial Trust for financing the research on which much of this chapter is based. Special thanks also go to the people in South Bristol who shared their experiences and ideas with me, and to Daphne Vaughan, Julie Swain and the individuals and families concerned for help with the pen-pictures.

References

Atkinson D and Ward L (1986) A part of the community: social integration and neighbourhood networks. London, Campaign for People with Mental Handicaps.

Atkinson D and Ward L (1987) Friends and neighbours. Relationships and opportunities in the community for people with mental handicap. In: Malin N (ed). Re-assessing community care. London, Croom Helm.

Humphreys S, Lowe K and de Paiva S (1986) Community care workers. Part 1. A description of the community care worker service in NIMROD. Cardiff, Mental Handicap in Wales Applied Research Unit.

Independent Development Council for People with Mental Handicap (1985) Living like other people. London, IDC.

Ward L (1984) Planning for people: developing a local service for people with mental handicap. 1. Recruiting and training staff (project paper 47). London, King Edward's Hospital Fund for London.

Ward L (1986) Alternatives to CMHTs: developing a community support service in South Bristol. In: Grant G, Humphreys S and McGrath M (eds). Community mental handicap teams: theory and practice. Kidderminster, British Institute for Mental Handicap.

Ward L (1987) Pursuing quality in community support services. Lessons from the Wells Road experience. In: Ward L (ed). Getting better all the time? Issues and strategies for ensuring quality in community services for people with mental handicap (project paper 66). London, King Edward's Hospital Fund for London.

Jan Porterfield

Promoting opportunities for employment

More and more people with learning disabilities want real jobs and increasing numbers are getting them. There is now consider-able evidence that many, including some who are severely handi-capped, are not only capable of working but, *when given appropriate support*, can work in open employment and are valued by their employers and colleagues as good workers.

ISSUES AND PRINCIPLES

The 'an ordinary life' initiative addressed the employment of people with learning disabilities in 1983 when the King's Fund established a working group to look at daytime occupation. The group (of which I was a member) began by discussing existing daytime services in adult training centres (ATCs), social education centres (SECs) and so on, their positive features and ways they could be improved. The discussion kept coming back to the fact that day centres were not very successful at meeting individual needs because they were usually expected to provide a wide range of conflicting services: work experience for skilled people, educational and recreational activities for others and physical care for people with severe and multiple handicaps. Day centres typically are expected to provide all things to all adults labelled as mentally handicapped: this seems to be an impossible task.

Gradually members of the working group narrowed their brief to finding ways in which those who wanted jobs could be helped to get them. The jump from day centres to open employment may seem a very big one. It was based on lengthy discussions of ideal daytime futures for people with learning disabilities, in the light of the philosophy of normalisation and the three key principles set out in the first *An Ordinary Life* discussion paper. Reviewing these basic principles led to two difficult questions:

Why is it acceptable for people with learning disabilities to live in ordinary houses but unacceptable for them to have ordinary jobs?

If we really believed that people with learning disabilities have the same rights and human value as everyone else, why were we discussing segregated daytime occupation?

WHY EMPLOYMENT?

Members of the group could not justify the daytime segregation of people with learning disabilities in any rational way. The question for us became not *whether* people with learning disabilities should have the same range of daytime options as other people, but *how* they could be helped to take advantage of the options available. We focused on employment because, even in times of high unemployment, having a job is the most valued daytime option for most people. Although we did not have all the answers, we felt the question (how can people with learning disabilities be helped to get jobs?) needed to be asked and the issue (the employment of people with learning disabilities) raised at the national level.

We knew of a few people with learning disabilities who were employed or getting unpaid work experience. (Some, especially those with severe and multiple disabilities, were in the United States.) This encouraged the group to focus on employment: if it were possible for a few people, it could be possible for many more.

Some members of the working group were more enthusiastic than others about the concept of 'an ordinary working life'. There were reservations about the practical details of finding enough jobs for the numbers of people currently attending day centres, those receiving no services, and those approaching school-leaving age. There were also fears that advocating 'an ordinary working life' would alienate staff working in existing day services by making them feel that their work was being criticised. As well, the National Development Group had recommended that adult training centres shift their focus away from work and towards social education (National Development Group 1977). This was a progressive, positive move and we hesitated to make any suggestion that might be interpreted as recommending a return to the boring and repetitive contract work that had so markedly decreased since the publication of the NDG pamphlet.

The shift in many ATCs and SECs to more stimulating and creative activities was welcomed, as was the move of many centre-based activities into community facilities such as colleges and leisure centres. Nevertheless, we felt that more could be done to encourage the integration of people with learning disabilities with non-handicapped people, and that working together in open employment was a good way of achieving this. We began to investigate the option of employment and, although we recognised that the discussion paper we were producing (*An Ordinary Working Life*, King's Fund 1984) would be controversial, we felt it needed to be written.

LOOKING AT EXAMPLES

The ideas of the group were discussed with a small number of ATC/SEC staff. Many, but not all, were keen to change their way of working, to be less constrained by the building and to help attenders move out from the centre into the wide range of community activities. Some had already begun to put these ideas into practice, but many did not know how or where to begin. This reaction was encouraging. We thought, however, that it would be helpful to supplement the discussion paper with some detailed descriptions of successful schemes or individuals. MENCAP's Pathway Employment Service was well known. But even this longstanding and successful service was not fully understood or appreciated. Various members of the group had heard about or visited one or two innovative schemes, but real knowledge was sketchy and somewhat inaccurate.

A grant from the Joseph Rowntree Memorial Trust made it possible to conduct a short study of employment schemes and services in Britain which promoted the integration of people with learning disabilities with non-handicapped people. (The fieldwork for this study was conducted by the author. Descriptions of many of the schemes, services and individuals visited can be found in *The Employment of People with Mental Handicap* (King's Fund 1985).) The study was not intended to be comprehensive, evaluative or to recommend any particular service or method; it was, rather, a review of what was happening. We hoped to stimulate interest and action by reporting successful attempts to find employment for people with learning disabilities.

At the beginning of the study, we thought that there would not be many places to visit. This prediction turned out to be pessimistic: there were many small-scale schemes in addition to two major initiatives (the Pathway Employment Service and the Shaw Trust). Among the places visited were a cooperative bakery, work experience schemes operating within day centres, youth training schemes, employment services especially for people with learning disabilities, a development officer from the Shaw Trust, two Pathway employment officers and a very severely handicapped woman who had become employed with the help of her residential staff.

All the visits were interesting and some were inspiring; they were also challenging because time after time I met people who had overcome tremendous odds to become employed. My view of the potential of people with learning disabilities radically changed as I talked to them, their employers and colleagues, and saw the work they were doing. People were doing so much more than anyone had thought possible. I was impressed by their courage and determination to succeed.

The 'job finders' were fascinating. The vast majority were attractive, well-dressed, articulate and had friendly, outgoing personalities. Many had no previous experience of working with people with learning disabilities and they did not see this as a disadvantage. In fact, some said they thought it was an advantage not to have the negative attitudes they found among many staff working in services. Many had experience in business or industry, and felt this to be a distinct advantage because it enabled them to talk to employers in their own language. They reminded me of good salespeople and many said they viewed their job as selling the concept of employing a person with learning disabilities to employers.

Most of the schemes and services I visited had been started because one individual was dissatisfied with existing day services. These people are innovators who saw the problems of these services (not enough places, segregation, people working for pocket money, people doing recreational activities that other adults do in their leisure time), had ideas for changing the service or starting a new one, and were able to convince someone in authority or a group with influence to help put these ideas into practice. None of these people felt they had all the answers but they were willing to try something different and all were achieving some measure of success.

COMMON THEMES

There were several common themes evident in the schemes I visited with implications for any new employment initiatives.

1 The number of services and schemes throughout Britain which are actively engaged in helping people with learning disabilities

to get jobs working alongside non-handicapped people has grown substantially since the project paper was published. Pathway and the Shaw Trust have both extended significantly, adding more 'job finders' and covering more of Britain. More day centres are establishing work experience programmes. Several authorities are focusing on employment as a real option for adults with learning disabilities. Several new schemes such as training cafés have been established and people are moving on from them into open employment. Many parent groups and voluntary organisations are also establishing their own employment schemes. Interest is increasing in helping people with severe learning disabilities to become employed, and at least one scheme (Rivermead Work Station in Sheffield) is involved in teaching a small group of severely handicapped people complicated assembly tasks.

It is surprising that these developments are occurring in a time of high unemployment. The emphasis on community services, the consciousness-raising activities of organisations such as CMHERA, CMH, the King's Fund, MENCAP and IDC, and the increased interest in citizen and self-advocacy may help to explain why this is happening.

There are still many challenges to be faced. The most important of these is maintaining the emphasis on integration. The pressure to congregate and segregate handicapped people continues. Employment services and schemes must be aware of these pressures and focus on their primary task of bringing handicapped and non-handicapped people together so that they can form personal relationships through work.

2 Many people with learning disabilities want to be employed and are able to do a job, given appropriate support.

3 Many people with 'problem behaviour' do not have these problems in the workplace.

4 Trying to predict whether someone will be able to do a job is hazardous. People need to have the opportunity to show what they can do in the workplace.

5 Many people change dramatically after they start working: they gain confidence and skills, and are happier and friendlier.

The people with learning disabilities I met during the study were highly motivated individuals. They wanted to work and to get away from being considered 'handicapped'. They had overcome staggering odds in order to become employed: being labelled as mentally handicapped; no expectation of achieving anything and no encouragement to think of employment as an option for adult life; no preparation for work at school; being institutionalised either in hospital, a hostel or by attending a day centre. Many also have physical problems (poor sight and/ or hearing, inability to speak or difficulty walking) or had come from disadvantaged family backgrounds and had been or were currently coping with relatives who had serious emotional problems.

6 Although some employers take on people with learning disabilities out of kindness, many later acknowledge that employing them makes good economic sense.

Many employers are hesitant about hiring someone who is labelled as 'mentally handicapped'. As with the general public, there is misunderstanding among employers about what mental handicap is and how it will affect the potential worker's performance. After taking on a person with learning disabilities, however, most find that the worker is punctual, reliable and efficient. Much of this depends on the choice of job (is it something the person really wants to do?), the help the person receives before becoming employed, the care that goes into on-the-job training and the support given following employment. The schemes and services that can provide this kind of attention are very successful at finding the right job for each person, thus making both the employer and the new employee 'satisfied customers'.

7 There is a great deal of misunderstanding and confusion about the benefit system. Staff, families and people with learning disabilities are concerned that once people start working they may be worse off financially or that it may be difficult to reclaim benefits if they become unemployed.

8 Some people with learning disabilities are paid very low wages so as not to interfere with their benefits. Some employers 'top up' low wages with goods, free transport, free meals, and so on.

These statements are as true today as they were in 1984. People are advised to seek individual guidance from their local DHSS office, but this is time-consuming and does not solve the general problem. The benefits system is a real disincentive to become employed. The situation as it stands also makes it easy to exploit workers who have learning disabilities. If the choice is a pitifully paid job or no job, many will opt for unfair pay.

There is an urgent need for a review of the benefits system as it relates to people with learning disabilities.

9   Although most could best be described as moderately or mildly handicapped, there are people with severe and multiple handicaps who are employed.

The best and most quoted example is Susan Walker (a pseudonym). Susan cannot hear, does not speak, is very partially sighted and has been labelled as 'severely mentally handicapped and behaviour disordered'. She lived in a locked ward of a mental handicap hospital for 30 years. At the time I visited her, she was working as a pub cleaner, but unfortunately the pub was closed by the small brewery that owned it. She now works part-time cleaning a dentist's surgery, for which she is paid the going rate.

When Susan Walker moved to a small house in the community, the staff became very committed to her and, on hearing that she was unwelcome at the local day centre, decided (astonishingly) to help her get a job. Since she appeared to like cleaning they looked for domestic work. Helping her find a job, learn the tasks involved and behave acceptably for a work situation was a very lengthy, difficult and challenging process. The staff feel it was all worthwhile. Susan appears to love her job. (Although she cannot speak, she indicates this with sign language and the enthusiasm with which she does her work.) She has widened her social contacts, become much more confident and skilled, and has money with which to buy things for her home and save for a holiday. (More details of her remarkable story can be found in *The Employment of People with Mental Handicap* (King's Fund 1985).)

The fact that there is only one nationally known example of a person with such serious disabilities who has a job may indicate the difficulty in helping people with very severe disabilities to work. It may also signify, however, a lack of motivation to help someone in this way. The fact that there is one person with Susan Walker's problems who is benefiting so obviously from the experience of work should motivate us to re-evaluate the potential of people with serious learning disabilities. Meeting Susan Walker and her staff and seeing her do her job and enjoy it so much, has convinced me not that she is an exceptional person but that the level of commitment of the staff helping her is exceptional. If others received such help, they too could achieve her success.

10 Most people with learning disabilities need help in order to find and keep a job. Some need only minimal support for a short period, while others need a great deal of support throughout their working lives. The level of support must be decided on an individual basis and constantly reviewed to meet the person's changing needs.

11 Working alongside non-handicapped people is a very good way for people with learning disabilities to become integrated into the community.

WAYS FORWARD

The challenge is to find ways of providing opportunities for adults with learning disabilities to experience the world of work at first hand. This will help them to make informed choices about whether they want to become employed and, if so, to decide the kinds of jobs they want. Some day centres have established work experience programmes together with job finding and support mechanisms. These programmes give people opportunities to try out various jobs in real workplaces, working anything from a few hours a day to five days a week. They receive no pay because work experience is short-term (a few weeks) and gives people an accurate idea of what various jobs are like. After several work experience placements, they are better able to decide the kinds of jobs they would like and efforts are made to help them get those jobs in open employment.

Often these schemes are linked with employment services, such as Pathway, Shaw Trust or the local disablement resettlement officer. In some centres one member of staff is responsible for the work experience scheme; in others a small group of staff or all those interested share the responsibility. Arrangements are made to enable those responsible for the scheme to have time away from the centre, visiting potential places of employment and supporting those doing work experience. In some centres staff cover for each other; in others volunteers help supervise groups alongside other members of staff. A few centres have now established work experience posts which allow a member of staff to concentrate on the scheme.

Experience has shown that it is best to start working with a very small number of people (one to five) who are particularly keen to get jobs: *motivation seems to be much more important than skill*. It is also important to discuss the scheme with the person's family if he or she lives with relatives, or residential staff if he or she lives in staffed accommodation. If relatives or staff are opposed to the scheme, it may be better to choose someone who has the support of those at home. Decisions about who to include need to be made according to individual circumstances.

In some areas schemes have been established specifically to provide work experience. An example of this is Applejacks, a café run by the Camden Society for People with a Mental Handicap and used by the general public in Camden Town. People receive training while working in the café from one to three days a week for several weeks or months. When it is felt that they are ready they are helped to find jobs in open employment.

Employment services outside the day centre structure have also been established in some places. Apart from the large services which operate in many parts of the country (Pathway and Shaw Trust), there are now a few small, local services run by statutory organisations (Blakes Wharf) or voluntary bodies (Welsh Initiative for Specialised Employment). These services specifically help people with learning disabilities to get jobs and support them in work. Ideally these services work in close collaboration with day centre staff and coordinate the help they give.

There is no one way forward and no single model of good practice that should be established everywhere. Each local area or group will need to find its own way (IDC 1985). Lessons can be learned from the experiences of others, but these need to inform practice rather than prescribe it. Adaptations need to be made to meet individual needs and local requirements.

Because most adults with learning disabilities have been segregated from other people, they have very different views of the possibilities for their lives. Until recently most have thought that their futures would be more of the same, spent as lifelong trainees. It was never clear to them – or anyone else – what they were training for. Work experience schemes and special employment services are necessary to help them to catch up, begin to understand the concept of employment and see it as a real option. Most people with learning disabilities will probably continue to need help in getting jobs and support in keeping them. However, we hope that they will not continue to see themselves as having futures which are different from those of others, and will have the same opportunities as other adults. If children with learning disabilities are educated alongside non-handicapped children in ordinary schools, they will be encouraged to think of employment as an option for them to the same extent that it is for their non-handicapped contemporaries. They will begin to view themselves as people of value and worth.

IQ doesn't indicate how well a person will do (in employment)... It's important to get people away from a 'handicapped environment'. Often people who have a bad track record – who cause trouble in ATCs and hostels – are my best clients. The ones who are stroppy have character. The 'good' ones have given up. *A job finder*

References

Independent Development Council for People with Mental Handicap (1985) Living like other people. London, IDC.

King's Fund (1984) An ordinary working life: vocational services for people with mental handicap (project paper 50). London, King Edward's Hospital Fund for London.

National Development Group for the Mentally Handicapped (1977) Day services for mentally handicapped adults (NDG pamphlet 5). London, DHSS.

Porterfield J and Gathercole C (1985) The employment of people with mental handicap: progress towards an ordinary working life (project paper 55). London, King Edward's Hospital Fund for London.

Alice Etherington, Keven Hall and Emma Whelan

What it's like for us

ALICE ETHERINGTON

Where I work

I get on quite well at the Charlie Ratchford Centre [a day centre for elderly people]. I work from 8.30–4pm full-time. I have been working on my own; it is very hard but I am getting used to it now. The manager of the buffet where I work supervises my work. Viv Davies [employment service] took me for the interview to get the job. She helps me if there are any problems.

I belong to NUPE. They wrote a letter for me about the fact that I was doing too much work. One of the care assistants is my stop steward. We have a staff meeting on Tuesday or Thursday, from 3–4pm once a week. We talk about cleaning the carpet and chairs in the buffet or about leaks in the buffet equipment. Next meeting we might talk about the advertisement for another person to help me.

Camden Social Services give me my wages. Two men bring our wages slips on Fridays. The wage is paid into the bank. I got a rise back in April – from £78 to £81. If there is anything wrong with the money, you see Pat [personnel manager]; she helps me with things like tax. I ask my supervisor first. Then pass it to Viv Davies. I put money in the bank and I keep back money for things like insurance, TV, rent. I have a new TV set which costs £6.95 per month. I save up money for holidays.

Before I got this job I kept looking in the Job Centre. I was trying to help myself. They tried but they couldn't get me anything.

I would like to stay at Charlie Ratchford. I would like to do more cooking but they say I can't till I've been on the cookery course. I like doing things like making tea and coffee and making bread and toast. I cook at home. I make sausage, bacon, eggs, chips and spaghetti bolognaise. My sister taught me to cook. Mum didn't allow me to cook very much. I am dying for the catering course! When someone else is employed with me at Charlie Ratchford, then I can go on the course. I hope to go on the Applejacks course.

Where I live

I live in a small group home. It has four bedrooms, a kitchen, garden, sitting room. I have a room of my own. Some of the furniture is mine; some came from CSMH.

I used to live in a group home with more people. But people asked me to do too many things for them. They didn't let me have any relaxation. I told CSMH I wanted to move out. I was given a choice of where I'd like to go and I said I'd like to go to Chetwynd Road. My friend Mary lives at Chetwynd Road. I went in for a few days first; then they said I could go in for a month. My support worker said I could look after myself; that I would be alright.

At the group home we share jobs; share the cooker and things. I have a key to the front door and to my bedroom. I like it there. I don't want to move. I wouldn't want to live on my own, in case I have any fits and nobody would know about it.

Holidays

I had a week off. I go out for the day – perhaps go to Brent Cross. The elderly people who go to Charlie Ratchford said they were dying of thirst while I was away! They were very glad to have me back. I give them extra cups of tea. I have been asking to go on holiday for years but my Mum and Dad are not keen. I would love to go on holiday. I have been asking for years to go on holiday with my family, but I can't because of this physical problem I've got. I have had the problem all my life. My Mum and Dad tried to get help with it when I was seven or ten but they couldn't do anything about it. I don't think I will get married because of it.

I went to hospital for an operation. I got Get Well cards from people. I used to go to hospital appointments on my own but I couldn't answer all the questions. Now my support worker goes with me if the appointment is in the morning, and my Mum if it is in the afternoon.

What I do in my spare time

I see my sister. She lives not too far away. I've got a bus pass, a train pass and a taxi card. I only use the taxi card for evening classes. Monday evening I go to sewing class, Tuesday evening pottery, Wednesday screenprinting, Saturday swimming. I have a leisure card so it doesn't cost me anything at the swimming. Sometimes I miss a class if I need to have an evening at home.

Viv Davies helped to get the pottery class. I went on my own for the sewing class. Another lady helped me to go to screenprinting. I might change this to cooking instead. On Thursdays I go to a class for spelling at the Working Men's College and then I go to Gateway Club. At Gateway Club I do knitting, sometimes sewing. All these things are at different places.

I like knitting and using a sewing machine. I like pottery and art. I am learning how to draw from a book. I like making things. I want to learn typewriting. I have a typewriter but it doesn't work; I am trying to get it fixed.

I like country dancing. I am going to Sunbury-on-Thames with the Salvation Army band. We are going with Mr Harris [club leader]. We are also going to Brighton by coach. This is organised by the social committee of CSMH.

KEVEN HALL

Getting a job

I would like to get a job at the new Sainsburys, taking shopping to the cars or doing the shelves or handing out the baskets. My Dad would help me get the job. I went myself to International to try for a job. The man told me he would find me something but I am still waiting. A friend of mine gets paid working with animals. Another friend had a job on a traffic patrol outside a school. I would like to work on a farm – on my brother's farm. My brother has got a nice farm. He works very hard on it. He breeds puppies and shire horses. His farm is in Little Heath, Potters Bar.

I do two paper rounds each week. It takes about an hour to do one round and we get paid £1 for each round. We just got a summer bonus. I have never done any work experience. My social worker can help me get a job but I haven't got a social worker at the moment.

Where I live

I live at home with my Dad. He used to be in the army but is retired now. I help my Dad with housework and shopping. I would like to cook but Dad is worried about my hurting myself. We do cooking at the Centre – we make shepherd's pie and cauliflower cheese. I make toasted ham sandwiches on the grill at home. I don't like it when the butter spatters.

Dad gives me money. He gives me 85p on Mondays, which includes my dinner money, £1 on Wednesday, £1.15 on Thursday and 25p on Tuesday and Friday. Dad helps me save up – in my

Anglia book. Dad puts the money in for me and helps me take money out too. My supplementary benefit book is in my name. If I had a job they would take my book away. Sometimes I don't get sickness benefit – even for a week's sickness.

My Dad is very helpful to me. I am living with my Dad to keep him company. I would like to live in Malta with my friends. When Dad dies I will go to live in Malta. My sister helps me. She invites me for dinner but I don't stay overnight.

What I do during the week

I go to the training centre on Mondays, Tuesdays and Fridays. I meet my key worker for ten minutes, 9.00–9.10 and also in the tutor group from 9.30–10. I go to Tracy at 10 then we do our shopping, have a cup of tea and make our dinner. At 1.30 I go to advanced workshop with Phoebe – we make wooden stools. At 3.50 we go home. I am assessed every six months. They say I am improving a lot – helping a lot. But they still say I am not ready for a job. It was a staff discussion – I wasn't there. My Dad doesn't go to the staff discussions – only to the case review. I get £4 a week at the training centre.

I go to Graham Park [FE College] on Wednesdays and Thursdays. We do drama on Wednesdays at 3pm. I like it. We are doing a Christmas play for the College and the public.

We do general studies – writing, numeracy, go to the library. We take books home from the library. I took one about Australia. We do social studies, prices, draw maps. I do typing – 14 words a minute. We work on computers. We do exercises which have questions and answers – Wordwize, Holidays. You have to be able to read to do the computers.

I like going there because I meet friends – different handicapped people. We meet other people before the morning classes. Some people do London life; some do sports training; some are on computer courses. We have dinner with other people but mostly sit with our own group. Sometimes we sit with other people. The staff sit with students in the canteen.

What I do in my spare time

I go to Never Never drama group on my own. I like to do sports – football and cricket. I used to go to a sports club at Golders Green. Now I go to a sport club called Stopwatch. We play unihock – it's a sort of hockey. Twelve people belong to Stopwatch. Barnet MENCAP organises it.

I played football last Friday and we won 6–2 against a team called Acton. I go to Watford Club with Ray from Broadfields ATC.

The Whetstone Outlook Sunday club meets at 4pm. It's a musical club with us playing musical instruments and singing songs. We also get together playing games, puzzles, pool. We also go on outings and we paint pictures.

I like helping at bazaars for MENCAP. I go and play bingo on Friday and Sunday evening.

Where I have lived

I went to a group home in East Finchley but I didn't like it because they didn't check up on me enough. I was at Woodley [1975] – we had our own keys to our dormitories and I used to get more money there – £25. Now it is only £4 a week. We used to make stuffed toys – Miss Piggy and Kermet. I also lived at Pengwyn Hall with Mr Weinberg and at Swaylands.

I liked Woodley best of all. There were all sorts of different people there. The oldest person was 72. We used to get up at 6am and clock on to start work at 8am. We didn't have far to go to the pub – just outside the back gate. I failed the test at the end because I was worried about my Mum being ill. Someone told me on the last day that I was worried about my Mum and Dad. There was no written report at the end. Someone told my Dad on the telephone that I wasn't working well. They also spoke on the phone to my social worker.

I would like to get my own place.

EMMA WHELAN

Where I work

I like work because it is useful and you learn things out. I help disabled people in their homes. I have been doing it a year and two weeks. I earn good enough wages but I think for the job we do we are entitled to more money. At the moment I am happy with it but later on I would like a job even better. A job without lifting, which is really tiring – perhaps a job working with children.

I went to the Job Centre, careers offices and looked in the newspaper. I think I got my job with Harrington [horticultural employment services] through the Job Centre. The Harrington helped me to get my job with Community Aide Programme. They have not asked me if I would like to do anything different.

The only person who could help me get a better job is my mum. I would not ask my social worker for anything. Harrington was my first job. I was twenty. I left school at seventeen and a half – then I went to college in Paddington. They helped me get the job at Harrington. I liked it at college – we did pottery, art, drama, computers, PE, cooking. We did not do enough reading and writing. I looked for a job in my dinner break. In the end the college helped.

I manage my money well and I save some – you have to these days. My pay is paid direct to Giro Bank every fortnight. They give me a slip. I am still paying emergency tax; my Mum is helping me sort this out. But at least it's helping me to save.

Where I live

I have my own flat in Camden and I really like it because it's quiet. I like being in private when I come in at night. This is the first time.

I want to stay here until I am too old to walk up the stairs. I went to the housing department. I found out where it was myself, and told them I was homeless and they put me on the list. I had to keep chasing them up until they did. Sometimes they were nice, sometimes not, and I gave them an earful! I can understand King's Fund letters, because you put easy words; but not the housing department, because they put difficult words.

Friends

A friend is someone you like who likes you. You like doing things together. I have some friends but not so many as I used to have. I like going out with them to a pub or whatever, or go back to their house. Some of my friends I met on the training course – one lives in Harlow. Most of my friends now are new friends. My old friends I don't see so much.

If I had more money I would like to go to the pictures and go on holiday abroad more. I like going to Spain. I would like to go with my friends.

I work five evenings up until 6 o'clock; sometimes later. I get home about half seven, depending on whether I walk or have my bike, so I don't have much time to do things in the evening.

At weekends I go to see my Mum or I go to see my friends. I have a bus pass – free on buses and undergrounds and half-fare on trains. I ring my Mum up nearly every day.

I am happy with life. I am really enjoying it; more than I did before.

95

Janet Maher and Oliver Russell

Serving people with very challenging behaviour

Some of the services developed over the past eight years have been firmly committed to meeting the needs of those who pose severe challenges because of the intensity or unpredictability of their behaviour. Many of these services have had to struggle to fulfil this commitment, however, and it is now apparent that the needs of such people may not be met by the pattern of services being planned in many parts of the country.

If appropriate services are to be developed and sustained then we have to consider whether the key principles of *An Ordinary Life* can provide the ground rules upon which they should be built, or whether the principles have to be modified in any way. As noted in the Introduction, these key principles are:

> People with learning disabilities have the same human value as anyone else.

> People with learning disabilities have a right and a need to live like others in the community.

> Services must recognise the individuality of people with learning disabilities.

As professionals directly involved in planning and delivering services to people with learning disabilities, we believe that these principles are relevant and can provide the basis for service development. In this chapter we explore some of the tasks which need to be undertaken in planning and shaping services for this group of clients.

What do we mean by 'challenging behaviour'?

The phase 'challenging behaviour' has recently come into use to describe the range of problems shown by those whose disturbed behaviour produces feelings of despair and hopelessness in those who care for them. It was first used by The Association for Persons with Severe Handicaps (TASH) and is now preferred to terms like 'problem behaviour' because it stresses that such behaviours represent challenges to those who provide services, rather than problems which individuals with learning difficulties carry around with them.

To understand why someone is upset or disturbed it is necessary to take into account social and biological factors. Sometimes it will be easy to pinpoint the precipitant of an episode of disturbance; at other times it will be virtually impossible to find a beginning or an end to the problems presented. In conditions such as autism where failure to achieve successful social adaptation has been lifelong, major problems in communicating with others are added to the basic learning disabilities.

Whatever the underlying reasons, those who run the services need not only to provide diagnoses but also to try to understand what lies behind the behavioural disturbance and find appropriate ways of responding to the challenges. Herbert Lovett (1985) has recently provided a stimulating and thought-provoking account of how we might begin to develop a meaningful understanding of what lies behind challenging behaviour.

There is, of course, a real danger that in using the phrase 'challenging behaviour' we shall end up simply substituting one set of labels for another, but there are many advantages to be gained from refashioning our perceptions of 'problem behaviour', 'behavioural disturbance' and 'disorder'. It is important to move away from the view of disturbance as something that is always located within a person to a more rounded perspective which views the person in their living situation.

Use of the term 'challenging behaviour' emphasises that our central concern should be with the adequacy of the services, which need to be made more responsive and effective. Any disturbance which an individual shows may, of course, have been initiated by pain, disease, grief or any of the other precipitants which cause suffering and distress. However, the disturbed behaviour will very often be maintained by processes that have little to do with the factors which first triggered the disturbance.

COPING WITH CHALLENGING BEHAVIOUR

Those who are most closely involved with individuals showing challenging behaviour will usually have exhausted all the avenues available to them. Although some live with their families or in residential homes, many people with highly challenging behaviour live in hospital wards. It may be helpful to indicate the broad categories of problems with which service providers have the most difficulty.

Challenging behaviour which persists over a long period of time

We might expect to find a history of problem behaviour in those who have, over a long period of time, failed to settle into their environment. Such people will often have had serious difficulties in communicating with others and may have had problems forming close relationships. Some may live at home but most will be found in a hospital ward or other institutional setting. Some will have had diagnostic labels such as 'autistic' applied to them, while others will have simply been seen as 'difficult' or 'aggressive'.

Examples of such behaviour may include: causing physical injury or damage to themselves, or to others (biting, pushing or striking); behaviour which might be construed as meddlesome or interfering; upsetting or offending others (for example, by undressing in a public place or making sexually explicit gestures) or being destructive (tearing clothes or damaging toys).

Intermittent episodes of disturbance

Episodic disturbance may be shown by those who, though generally able to meet the demands of daily life may, often at unpredictable moments, become upset and disturbed for reasons that are not always immediately understood. Explanations for such episodes may only emerge over the course of time. The range and types of disturbance shown may be similar to those described above.

Emotional disturbance

Because it may be difficult to obtain an accurate account of the disturbed person's own feelings, staff and family members may have to make their own judgment about the reasons for a particular episode of emotional upset. Factors such as grief, anger and sexual frustration may trigger disturbance. People with severe learning disabilities experience frustration, failure, incomprehension and humiliation. It is not surprising that their feelings may sometimes get on top of them and cause them to react explosively or unpredictably to new situations.

Psychiatric disorder

Although it is more difficult to diagnose psychiatric illness in people with a learning disability, it is important to recognise that some of the most severe behavioural disturbances may be manifestations of a psychiatric disorder. For example, the onset of a hypomanic illness may be marked by restlessness, inability to sleep, boisterousness, lack of inhibition and irritability. The onset of a schizophrenic illness may be accompanied by strange and unusual behaviour that is not immediately understood but which greatly impairs an individual's ability to relate normally to other people. Whether people with a learning disability are more or less likely than other people to suffer from psychiatric disorders is still not resolved.

Sensory impairment

Those who have severe visual or auditory impairments are particularly vulnerable to social isolation. If these problems are not recognised, their social difficulties may be enhanced. They may make strenuous efforts to make themselves understood and if no one is able to interpret their demands, they may express their frustration in a way which is seen by others as disturbance or disorder.

THE SIZE OF THE PROBLEM

In 1976 the Office of Population, Censuses and Surveys was asked by the Jay committee (Great Britain, Parliament 1979) to survey the extent of problem behaviour occurring in people with severe learning disabilities. OPCS estimated that 25 per cent of adults and 50 per cent of children in mental handicap hospitals had some form of behaviour problem which was sufficiently marked and consistent to be recorded as such by the staff. This OPCS study found that in residential homes 7 per cent of the adults and 34 per cent of the children were reckoned to be behaviourally disturbed.

Behavioural disturbance is not the same as psychiatric disorder and where studies aimed at determining the prevalence of psychiatric disorder have been carried out the prevalence rates have often been higher than those just quoted. This may reflect the fact that the psychiatric survey will have identified individuals who are depressed (and therefore psychiatrically ill) but who are not showing problem behaviour. Some surveys of hospital populations have been limited to psychiatric disorder, while others have cast their net more widely.

A census of mental handicap hospitals carried out in 1972 found that 16 per cent of the residents suffered from severe psychiatric disorder (Department of Health and Social Security 1972), while Reid (1983) estimated that around 50 per cent of the

99

population of a mental handicap hospital pose significant management problems because of psychiatric disorder. However, after Ineichen (1984) had reviewed the evidence on which Reid had based his estimate, an agreement was reached between them that the prevalence figure of 16 per cent quoted in the DHSS census was probably nearer the correct figure than Reid's earlier estimate (Reid 1984). Day (1983) also considers that the prevalence of psychiatric disorder is much higher and found in his study that 50 per cent of people with severe learning disabilities in hospital have an overlay of psychiatric disorder.

Although our information about the size of the problem in the community is far from complete it can be assumed that a considerable number of adults and children with severe learning disabilities whom we might describe as showing challenging behaviour are living at home and being looked after by their families.

In the ENCOR programmes in the United States 81 persons (7.7 per cent of the total of 1,045 served by the programme) were identified as having a dual diagnosis of severe learning disability and mental illness to such a degree as to require special supports and services. Of these, 22 presented severely disturbed behaviour on a daily basis and required an intense degree of support (Casey *et al* 1985).

A study carried out in Bristol in 1980 (Russell and Hall 1980) using the Wessex rating scale (Kushlick *et al* 1973) showed a similar prevalence of challenging behaviour. Severe behaviour disorder among adults with learning disabilities was reported in 7 per cent of those living with their families compared with 18 per cent among those in residential care. (Among children living with their families in Bristol in 1980 the rate of severe behaviour disorder was 16 per cent).

Extrapolating from the Bristol findings we might expect to find, within a total population of 100,000, ten children and 30 adults exhibiting behavioural disturbance on a daily basis which would be rated as severe on the Wessex Disability Scale and a further group of children and adults who manifest such behaviour from time to time.

Impotence and despair are the common ingredients in the situations of those who manifest challenging behaviours. The consequent stress is likely to disrupt family life and staff support. The needs which these individuals have for affection are difficult to supply and those who work with them are themselves often unsupported and undervalued.

MODELS FOR SERVICE DESIGN

Hospitals have always played a key role in services for people with challenging behaviour. In the past, disturbed or secure wards were commonplace. As commitment to locally based services increases, so does concern in some professionals and families that 'an ordinary life' will not work for people with challenging behaviour who will need residual hospital or specialist units. Reid (1983), looking at a group of mentally handicapped people with severe behavioural problems in hospital, found little evidence of improvement over a period of six years. He concluded that, although considerable resources had been invested in the services for these people, the problematic behaviours seemed impervious to any type of intervention. Carter (1984), researching reasons for admission to a mental handicap hospital over a ten-year period, found that over half the admissions were because the behaviours of the mentally handicapped people could not be coped with in community settings with the support services then available.

TYPES OF SPECIALIST UNIT

The research literature would indicate that at least three types of specialist unit have been advocated:

a) a residual hospital unit for people whose behaviour is considered unamenable to any intervention and far too challenging for community living;
b) a psychiatric assessment/treatment unit for those in whom severity of psychiatric disorder warrants admission to hospital;
c) a specialist training unit for people whose behaviour is amenable to change within a strict behavioural management regime.

Specialist provision is also needed for those who have committed offences and may therefore be subject to restrictions under the 1983 Mental Health Act. It may be difficult to meet the needs of these individuals outside of a specialist unit since, although they may not necessarily show challenging behaviour, they may require psychiatric treatment and secure accommodation. Whether or not segregated hospital accommodation is necessary continues to be debated.

Although there is support for specialist hospital units, particularly from psychiatrists (Day 1983, Shapiro 1974, Royal College of Psychiatrists 1986), there are drawbacks which must be considered. Once a client is removed from his or her natural environment reintegration after treatment can be problematic. Even if treatment within the specialist unit is successful, considerable resources are needed within the community to ensure a smooth return. Placing people with challenging behaviour together in the same unit can also be problematic. New challenging behaviour can be learned unless the regime is very structured and strict. As proponents of 'an ordinary life' we would argue that such units only contain and control, and do not enable people to develop skills and an understanding of their own worth.

MANAGING CHALLENGING BEHAVIOUR IN ORDINARY SETTINGS

There is, however, a model of service design built on the belief that anyone with learning disabilities can live in the community given appropriate resources, including the option of being referred to the appropriate specialist psychiatric or clinical psychology service skilled in the treatment and management of such behaviour.

There are a number of individual case studies which demonstrate that this model is possible. During 1981, ENCOR in the USA were able to maintain a few people with challenging behaviour in ordinary settings in the community (Casey *et al* 1985). They describe people with challenging behaviour as 'disconnected' individuals who have learned to control an otherwise meaningless world by inconsistently responding to or withdrawing from it. An effective approach to such people has focused on gaining control while tolerating, in a passively supportive but firm way the initial barrage of inappropriate behaviours.

Mansell (1980) describes a successful intervention with a young woman moving out of hospital. In Bristol and Weston Health Authority and in the NIMROD service in Cardiff some experience has been gained in managing challenging behaviour in ordinary settings.

However, most of the documented studies were small-scale – four being the largest number of clients involved – and were sufficiently supported by trained personnel. The viability of planning district-wide services using this model has been questioned given the limited resources available overall.

The major problem with this model of service design is the lack of a fall-back position. There will always be some occasions when challenging behaviour cannot be managed at home. For example, parents may no longer be able to cope with physical aggression directed towards them, or fellow residents in a community home may not tolerate someone breaking up the furniture. If the situation in the natural environment breaks down, is hospital the only solution?

AN ALTERNATIVE APPROACH

To achieve an effective service for people with challenging behaviour, the deficits of the first two models must be eliminated. We are developing a third model (Bristol and Weston Health Authority 1986) with three design elements:

1 staffing flexibility in the form of one-to-one teams
2 alternative respite care facilities
3 on-call advice from community-based specialists

It has already been established that the frequency and degree of challenging behaviour fluctuates, both for individuals and across a district. One-to-one teams, supernumerary to established staffing levels, provide the flexibility needed. These teams of highly trained staff provide a mobile workforce to assist, supplement, and if necessary take over, in the client's environment, be it an adult training centre, school, family home or hostel. In an earlier report (Maher 1987) we described the successful use of one-to-one teams with two clients, in one case to prevent admission to a specialist unit from another hospital ward, and in the second to prevent admission to a secure facility a considerable distance from the family home.

To provide one-to-one support on a 24-hour basis each team requires a minimum of four staff. The number of teams required in a district service would depend on the number of individuals needing this level of support.

The second element in this model is the respite care facility. Respite care for people with challenging behaviour could be provided either in the main house of an ordinary short-term care facility or in an adapted annexe, depending upon the frequency and intensity of the behaviour. One-to-one teams can accompany the client and provide support in either setting. The advantage of the separate annexe is that clients receiving short-term care in the main house are not disrupted. The closeness of the annexe allows for integrated activities when possible and gives the one-to-one staff access to colleagues in the main house. Special adaptations may be required in the annexe for walls, windows and doors to withstand some of the rough treatment they are likely to sustain.

The third element in the design is the availability of input from clinical psychologists and psychiatrists based in the community who are able to provide a 24-hour on-call service.

The service being developed in Bristol and Weston is not unique. Many of those who contributed to the King's Fund working party on *Facing the challenge: an ordinary life for people with learning difficulties and challenging behaviour* (King's Fund, 1987), are planning to develop and mount similar types of service in different parts of the country.

In conclusion, we believe that it is possible to meet the needs of those who present challenging behaviour within the context of the philosophy of 'an ordinary life'. Creating the services to do this requires the development of new ways of providing support to families and staff. This is perhaps the most important challenge facing services at the present time.

References

Bristol and Weston Health Authority (1986) Mental handicap services: a plan for implementation. Bristol and Weston DHA.

Blunden R and Allen D (eds) (1987) Facing the challenge: an ordinary life for people with learning difficulties and challenging behaviour (project paper 74). London, King Edward's Hospital Fund for London.

Carter G (1984) Why are the mentally handicapped admitted to hospital? A ten-year survey. British Journal of Psychiatry 145: 283–88.

Casey K, McGee J, Stark J and Menolascino F (1985) A community-based system for the mentally retarded: the ENCOR experience. Lincoln, Nebraska, University of Nebraska Press.

Day K (1983) A hospital-based psychiatric unit for mentally handicapped adults. Mental Handicap 11: 137–40.

Department of Health and Social Security (1972) Census of mentally handicapped patients in hospital in England and Wales at the end of 1970. London, HMSO.

Great Britain, Parliament (1979) Report of the committee of enquiry into mental handicap nursing and care. (Chairman Peggy Jay). (2 vols) Cmnd 7468. London, HMSO.

Ineichen B (1984) Prevalence of mental illness among mentally handicapped people: a discussion paper. Journal of the Royal Society of Medicine 77: 761–65.

Kushlick A, Blunden R and Cox G R (1973) A method of rating behavioural characteristics for use in large-scale surveys of mental handicap. Psychological Medicine 3: 466–78.

Lovett H (1985) Cognitive counselling and persons with special needs. New York, Praeger.

Maher J (1987) Ensuring quality in services for people with challenging behaviour. In: Ward L (ed). Getting better all the time? Issues and strategies for ensuring quality in community services for people with mental handicap (project paper 66). London, King Edward's Hospital Fund for London.

Mansell J (1980) Susan: the successful resolution of a 'severe behaviour disorder' with a mentally handicapped young woman in a community setting. In: Walton R G and Elliott D (eds). Residential care: a reader in current theory and practice. Oxford, Pergamon Press.

Reid A H (1983) Psychiatry of mental handicap: a review. Journal of the Royal Society of Medicine 76: 587–92.

Reid A H (1984) Prevalence of mental illness among mentally handicapped people. Journal of the Royal Society of Medicine 77: 894–95.

Royal College of Psychiatrists (1986) Psychiatric services for mentally handicapped adults and young people. Bulletin of the Royal College of Pyschiatrists 10: 321–22.

Russell O and Hall V (1980) Mental handicap and functional disability: a survey of disablement of mentally handicapped people from one health district. Research report no 6. Bristol, University of Bristol Department of Mental Health.

Shapiro A (1974) Fact and fiction in the care of the mentally handicapped. British Journal of Psychiatry 125: 286–92.

Roger Blunden

Safeguarding quality

It is clear from earlier chapters that the successful development of new services is itself a learning experience. It is important, therefore, that we provide safeguards to ensure that quality, once achieved, is maintained. Service development should be a *dynamic* process with a capacity for rectifying weaknesses and making further improvements. This chapter explores ways in which those providing services can constantly question what they are doing, learn from their experience and incorporate these lessons into practice.

It is not always clear what is meant by 'a high quality service' since different people will have different notions of quality. A useful starting point, therefore, is to clarify what a quality service might look like in practice.

In the discussion which follows we are concerned with the wide range of community-based services described earlier which support people either in their own homes or in residential accommodation in the community and provide access to education, work or leisure. While all these forms of service provision have different aims, there are some characteristics which quality services might be expected to have in common.

ACCESSIBILITY

One important set of characteristics comes under the heading of 'accessibility'. Does a particular form of service exist locally? How easy is it for users to find out about it? Is it easy to contact? Is it located within easy reach? Is there sufficient service to meet users' demand for it? Are the staff welcoming, friendly and helpful? In chapter 3, Philippa Russell highlights the need for services for children and their families to be readily accessible and well co-ordinated.

These aspects of service quality are all vitally important. Many problems with existing services stem from deficiencies in accessibility. For example, there are gaps in service provision. Many parts of the UK do not have adequate respite services, or the availability of community residential services is limited, or there is little further education available to people with learning disabilities. Often specialist services such as speech therapy or physiotherapy are in short supply.

Where a service does exist, it may be remote, difficult to contact, or not particularly welcoming to users. From recent discussions with families with a disabled member it is clear that many experience just these sorts of problems when dealing with some social security offices. They have great difficulty in finding out their eligibility for benefits, and in some cases have to go to extraordinary lengths to obtain their entitlement. These examples contrast with the notion of an accessible service, readily available and offering a welcoming face to its users.

EFFECTIVENESS

While all these features are important characteristics of a service's quality, they say nothing about the effectiveness of the service in meeting its users' needs. Even where a service exists locally and is readily accessible, this is no guarantee that it is effectively resolving the problems which its users present. There is perhaps an analogy with other services, such as a solicitor's office. It may be there, offer ready appointments and have a friendly receptionist, but this says nothing about its ability to offer effective legal advice.

So what is effectiveness in the context of services for people with learning disabilities? Because services aim to help people with almost every aspect of life, it is often quite difficult to give a specific answer to this question. However, one useful view of service aims has been set out by John O'Brien (1987). O'Brien suggests that there are five important ways in which services for people with learning disabilities should affect their users' lives.

1 *Community presence*

Services should enable their users to live and spend time within their local community. This applies to all aspects of life – home, work, education, leisure. One measure of a service's effectiveness would be the extent to which its users spend their time in settings where they have the opportunity to mix with other non-handicapped people.

2 *Relationships*

As well as providing opportunities to mix with other people, services will be effective to the extent that their users are helped to form relationships.

107

3 *Choice*

An effective service will also extend the range of choices available to those who use it. In the past, services have often restricted the choices available to their users, both in terms of everyday preferences like what to eat or what to wear, and major decisions such as where to live and with whom.

4 *Competence*

An effective service will support its users in learning and making use of new skills relevant to their living situation. They should experience a growing ability to perform useful and meaningful activities with whatever assistance is required.

5 *Respect*

It has often been the case that people with learning disabilities have been treated as second class citizens and denied the respect that is afforded to most members of society. Effective services will seek to reverse this process and ensure that their users are promoted as valued people in their own right.

These five factors provide a useful starting point to a discussion of service effectiveness. They help pinpoint ways in which we might expect to see quality services influencing the lives of those who use them in line with the original principles of the 'an ordinary life' initiative and provide a practical basis for examining service effectiveness. They also feature prominently in many of the examples given earlier in this book. Each writer has stressed community presence, where people with learning disabilities have been actively supported in spending time in a wide range of community settings. The importance of community presence is vividly illustrated in the chapter by Alice Etherington, Keven Hall and Emma Whelan, each of whom places a great deal of emphasis on contacts and friendships. In Chapter 5, Linda Ward has illustrated the way that services can take positive action to develop friendships, relationships and opportunities for participation in the local community. The services in Camden and Southwark described by Ritchard Brazil and Nan Carle stress the choices made available to individual users. Jan Porterfield illustrates many of the ways in which services increase the respect afforded to individuals by supporting them in proper paid work.

LESSONS FROM COMMERCIAL ORGANISATIONS

Of course the issue of quality is not unique to services for people with learning disabilities. Other organisations face the same problems of attempting to keep abreast of change, adapting to a changing environment and keeping their customers satisfied. As a commercial organisation has to justify its existence by making a profit, a service must benefit its users, or at least avoid causing them harm. The concern in the past has often been to avoid the scandals which have arisen due to some of the worst examples of neglect. However, the more positive philosophy of 'an ordinary life' has led to more critical questioning of the aims and achievements of service systems.

Beyond simply justifying their existence, many people seek to maximise the effectiveness of the organisation for which they work. This implies a constant questioning of whether the best is being achieved with the resources available. As new methods of working are developed, they need to be incorporated into the way in which the service is delivered.

In recent years a great deal has been written about the pursuit of quality in commercial organisations. Indeed, there is something of a cult in books offering advice on the pursuit of excellence. These draw on the experience gained in a range of companies and highlight key features of successful organisations. *In Search of Excellence* (Peters and Waterman 1982) draws attention to a number of characteristics of successful organisations. Although there may not be a direct comparison between American companies and services for people with learning disabilities in Britain, the book's description of an organisational culture in which quality is promoted in a number of ways may be useful in offering a vision of an appropriate service organisation.

The quality-conscious service would have an explicit set of values informing the way in which the organisation ran on a day-to-day basis. These values would emphasise the importance of the consumer (customer). Quality would be given priority by everyone from the most senior managers to front-line workers. Managers at all levels would make a point of maintaining contact with consumers, treating their views and problems as items of key concern. The focus of the organisation would be on results, not process. The organisational structure would be fluid in nature, with small groups and task forces being formed around the solution of particular problems. The formal structure of the organisation would not be allowed to get in the way of achieving results. Staff would be actively encouraged to innovate and to champion new ideas. There would be recognition that not all new ideas would succeed – failure would be tolerated and lessons learned from the experience. Peters and Waterman create the image of a highly motivated workforce with ample scope and encouragement to pursue the clearly-defined aims of the organisation. They use the term 'simultaneous tight-loose properties' to describe the way in which people within the organisation are given maximum individual autonomy within the context of firm central direction.

Many services present a very different picture from this image of an accessible action-oriented and quality-conscious organisation. Is this an unrealistic vision, or are there ways in which this notion of quality can be built into services for people with learning disabilities?

PURSUING QUALITY WITHIN SERVICE ORGANISATIONS

One set of ideas for helping to ensure that quality is 'built in' to the service system has recently been promoted by the Independent Development Council for People with Mental Handicap in their booklet *Pursuing Quality* (Independent Development Council 1986). This set out to provide practical guidance to people concerned with service quality. The IDC start by assuming that a number of conditions will need to be met if a service is to effectively review its quality and take steps to improve it.

The first is that key 'stakeholders' should be involved in defining and reviewing service quality. A stakeholder is anyone with a major interest in the service in question. Stakeholders are likely to include service users, family members, front-line staff, other professionals and managers, and may also involve representatives of the wider community such as local residents or politicians. It is argued that all these people have a key interest in the quality of the service and will be directly affected by attempts to produce change. Their active participation will help ensure that their interests are respected and that any decisions made are likely to be put into practice.

Philippa Russell has already stressed the importance of parents as stakeholders in services for young children. The Camden service, described in Chapter 4, shows how people with learning disabilities themselves can be actively involved in the decisions which affect their lives. Chapter 7 shows that people who use services have very firm views about the sort of help they require and, given the opportunity, will articulate these very clearly.

The second feature of an effective approach to service quality is that the service should be based upon a clear statement of values which is accepted and understood throughout the organisation. There should be a strong sense of mission, reflecting both the commitment to users as valued human beings and a clear direction in terms of the sort of impact the service sets out to have on people's lives. Again, earlier chapters have illustrated this: many of the services described have very clear statements of the values on which they are based and devote considerable effort to building the commitment of staff to those values.

This is not easy to achieve in practice. Written commitment to the value of clients as individuals may not inform the everyday practices of those working in the service or who take important policy or funding decisions. A general commitment to the status of service users is no guarantee that those involved have a clear sense of direction. However, it is difficult to envisage how a service might actively pursue quality in the absence of a clear notion of what it is seeking to do for its clients!

This notion of a clear sense of direction is pursued in the third of the IDC's suggested requirements. They introduce the term 'accomplishment', which was first coined in this context by Thomas Gilbert (1978). Gilbert makes the point that it is important to distinguish between what people do (their behaviour) and the effects of their actions on the world (their accomplishments). Thus in reviewing the quality of a service, it is the impact of that service on the lives of its users which is of real importance, not the process by which the service is delivered. Too many existing monitoring schemes concentrate on the process of service delivery, for example looking at numbers of clients served or bed occupancy rates, rather than accomplishments in terms of client outcome. It is unusual to see services being reviewed in terms of the extent to which they enable clients to expand their social relationships or learn and effectively use new skills. In contrast, the services described in this volume have stressed the outcomes for their users, for example extending their choices, expanding competence, enabling them to hold down respected jobs and to sustain relationships.

The fourth suggestion from the IDC is that any system of reviewing quality should be geared for action. A common criticism of many methods of monitoring services is that they are divorced from action. Information is collected and passed 'up' the system but little, if anything, happens as a result of this information. The IDC wanted to devise an approach to service quality in which the process of reviewing quality is directly linked to decisions about the practical steps to be taken to improve it.

The process suggested by the IDC is somewhat analogous to the individual plan system (Blunden 1980) which now forms the basis of much work with individual service users. It involves a group of people with a common interest in the service coming together to review its strengths and needs and on this basis setting goals for action. Meetings are held at regular intervals to review progress and agree further action goals. Whereas the individual plan approach applies to individual service users, the 'quality action' approach of the IDC relates to the entire service. In this way it resembles the notion of 'quality circles' (see for example Dewar 1980) which is prevalent in certain industrial organisations and becoming increasingly popular within the National Health Service.

QUALITY ACTION: A PRACTICAL APPROACH

In this approach, outlined in Figure 2, a working group of 'stakeholders' is formed specifically for the purpose of reviewing the service's quality and taking action to improve it. Such a group might operate at any level within a service system. It may be concerned with a particular service component (such as one residence or a domiciliary support service), a local community-based service having a number of components, or an entire service system operating over several localities.

The group first attempts to clarify the values behind its service. For some services this will be simply a question of reviewing the relevant documentation and ensuring that all members of the group are familiar with it. For others, where there is no clearly stated and accepted value base, this may be a longer process of thought and negotiation. The group also needs to consider the practical implications for service users of these values. This involves becoming clear about the service's 'accomplishments'. How does the service set out to affect its users' lives? This is a crucial step because it forms the basis of future reviews of the quality of service delivered.

The group then begins a circular process. Focusing on a specific accomplishment, the group sets out to find out how successful the service is. This will involve collecting evidence from records, conversations with users and staff, informal observation, or more formal evaluative activities, such as surveys of users. The group

Figure 2   The quality action process

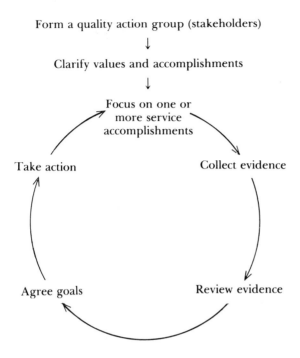

then reviews the evidence to determine the service's strengths and needs. This may well show gaps in the service or areas where improvements could be made. On this basis the group agrees goals for further action. Action may be at several levels. For example, front-line staff may identify ways in which they can change their day-to-day methods of working. There may be implications for staff training and a service manager may be able to take responsibility for these. High-level management or policy decisions may be needed and the group will need to identify responsibilities for negotiating these. It may not always be possible to identify appropriate action, or it may prove difficult to put this into practice because of financial or other constraints. However, the group's role is to achieve what it can and to ensure that action beyond its scope is placed on the relevant agendas.

The goals set by the group should be specific and individuals given responsibility to achieve them. At a later meeting the group will review the action taken and continue the quality action cycle, perhaps moving on to a new service accomplishment.

MAINTAINING QUALITY IN PRACTICE

The procedures outlined here seem little more than common sense. It might be argued that any service with ambitions of quality should be doing something like this as a matter of course. However, from the interest shown in the IDC document and the experience obtained while piloting the ideas, it appears that the simple notions outlined here are not a standard feature of good practice. Indeed, all of the organisations who helped the pilot work found that considerable commitment and effort were required in order to put these activities into practice.

For many people the business of delivering services is extremely time-consuming and leaves little opportunity for the review described above. It may not be easy to assemble a group which is representative of all the service's major stakeholders and which shares a common notion of the values underlying the service. The group's meetings need to be well-planned and structured if all participants are to make a useful contribution. There may be particular challenges in finding ways in which people with learning disabilities themselves can participate meaningfully in the group's work. However, experience with service organisations suggests that all these difficulties can be overcome where there is a strong commitment to the notion of pursuing quality within the service.

Ways of sustaining this effort also require some thought. It may be relatively easy to interest an organisation in piloting a new approach to service quality, but what happens when the novelty wears off? Ways need to be found to ensure that the issue of quality is always high on the agenda and that staff and others receive full recognition of their efforts in this direction. The lesson from the American commercial experience discussed above is that senior management has a major responsibility to ensure that a commitment to quality pervades the culture of the organisation. How often in most service organisations do senior managers concern themselves with the details of how the service is influencing the lives of its users?

In a follow-up to *In Search of Excellence*, Peters and Austin, in a book called *A Passion for Excellence* (1985) discuss the practical implications for managers of adopting the management style described in the earlier book. These include the notion of 'management by wandering about', in which managers ensure that they spend time routinely with customers and with people at all levels in the organisation. In services for people with learning disabilities this would involve managers regularly meeting service users and their families and talking with them about the important issues from the users' perspective. Managers might also spend time with staff and clients in various service settings. This would both sensitise them to staff issues and enable them to get some notion of how service users spend much of their lives.

Peters and Austin also discuss how managers in 'excellent' organisations take exceptional care of their customers. In our context, this would be reflected by managers showing a major commitment to the well-being of individual service users and responding to complaints or concerns expressed by them. Such managers constantly innovate and try new ways of improving their service, recognising that not all new ideas will bear fruit and learning from the experience gained.

The focus of the approach to quality action outlined here is on internal review. The group consists of people with a strong interest in the service. At some stage it will also be useful to involve outsiders in the review process. This gives fresh insights and can lead to constructive questioning of some of the ways of operating which are taken for granted. Thus the quality action process described here can be supplemented by an annual review using outside evaluators or a facilitator from outside the service organisation. For example, some services make a point of contracting a different form of external review each year. This may include a PASS evaluation (Wolfensberger and Glenn 1975) or an external evaluation, workshop, or 'programme design session' for staff and service users conducted by an outside consultant.

This approach has been primarily used at the front line of service delivery. While managers have been involved, the immediate concern has been with the patterns of working of front-line staff. The IDC envisaged that its approach would be applied equally at other levels, for example by the relevant managers at county or district level. The ideal would be various interlinking quality action groups with the same goals but operating from their own perspectives in the organisation. For example, a group at county level would be concerned with the broad impact of the service in terms of the numbers of clients supported in various living situations, while local groups would concentrate on more detailed assessment of service quality.

In this chapter we have examined the notion of quality in the context of services for people with learning disabilities. Unlike many commercial organisations which can easily measure the quality of their products in concrete terms, it is often difficult to define quality in terms of the impact of services on people's lives. However, there is much to be said for the notion of a service organisation's culture being centred around the quality of its users' lives.

The Independent Development Council's initiative 'pursuing quality' has been cited as one example of an approach which attempts to ensure that the issue of quality remains high on the organisation's agenda. This is one way in which quality can be regularly reviewed by key stakeholders in terms of the impact of the service on its users' lives and in ways which lead to practical improvements.

There is clearly a long way to go before services for people with learning disabilities are able uniformly to maintain quality at a high level. However, the development of new initiatives along the lines set out in *An Ordinary Life* and illustrated in this volume create both the opportunity and the necessity to ensure that the issue of quality is given a high priority as new services, oriented towards improving the lives of their users, are developed.

References

Blunden R (1980) Individual plans for mentally handicapped people: a draft procedural guide. Cardiff, Mental Handicap in Wales Applied Research Unit.

Dewar D L (1980) The quality circle guide to participation management. Englewood Cliffs, New Jersey, Prentice-Hall.

Gilbert T F (1978) Human competence: engineering worthy performance. New York, McGraw-Hill.

Independent Development Council for People with Mental Handicap (1986) Pursuing quality; how good are your local services for people with mental handicap? London, IDC.

O'Brien J (1987) A guide to personal futures planning. In: Bellamy G T and Wilcox B (eds). A comprehensive guide to the activities catalog: an alternative curriculum for youth and adults with severe disabilities. Baltimore, Paul H Brookes.

Peters T and Austin N (1985) A passion for excellence: the leadership difference. London, Collins.

Peters T J and Waterman R H (1982) In search of excellence: lessons from America's best-run companies. New York, Harper & Row.

Wolfensberger W and Glenn L (1975) PASS 3: a method for the quantitative evaluation of human services. Toronto, National Institute on Mental Retardation.

Part Three

ACHIEVING LARGE-SCALE CHANGE

Chris Gathercole, Tom McLean and David Whalley

Generating policy and action

This chapter is a case study of changes which have taken place in recent years in services in Lancashire and Greater Manchester, the area covered by the North Western Regional Health Authority (population four million). It tells of the growing interest in an ordinary life for people with learning disabilities at one of the region's large long-stay hospitals and the first few years of a developing community service in its home catchment district. The story is told from the point of view of a hospital and health service rather than, say, a family or social services department. This is because in the North West, the key initiatives which led to large-scale changes arose within hospitals and the health service.

METAMORPHOSIS OF AN INSTITUTION

Perhaps the most significant precursor of the shift from hospital to community living in the North West was the arrival in 1966 at Calderstones, a large mental handicap hospital near Burnley in Lancashire, of a new consultant psychiatrist. He began by guiding the hospital social work department in developing activities in the community such as employment, and later through an extensive holiday programme and shopping in the community. The number of residents at that time was almost 2,000; by late 1986 it had fallen to below 850.

In 1969 the Salmon reorganisation of nursing management was introduced at Calderstones. Between then and 1973, when the first chief nursing officer left, nursing services were dramatically reoriented. Residents came to be seen as individuals with their own interests, needs and rights. This may hardly seem worth mentioning nowadays, but the history of large long-stay hospitals tells of the needs of residents having been a very secondary consideration to the needs of others such as staff, parents, policy makers and the public. It took a major shift in basic assumptions before the needs of residents achieved priority. Since 1969 the job description of every nurse, at all levels in the hospital, has included 'encouraging the recognition of the resident as an individual'. Later, standards emphasising the rights and individuality of residents were spelt out in nursing procedure notes, with explanations as to why these are important.

In 1970, a 'seek and find' scheme encouraged staff in small mixed groups – social worker, nurse, consultant, administrator – to visit services elsewhere to find out what they could bring back to Calderstones. Seeking images of possibility from what is best in the world for people with learning disabilities has continued to challenge new generations of staff to strive for excellence. It has also served to weaken the boundaries which characterise rigid organisations, allowing information and ideas to flow in from the world outside and generating a dynamism for change. From then on, change became endemic. The word 'hospital' was dropped from the Calderstones name. Nurse uniforms were abandoned. Doctors extracted themselves from institutional management.

In the same year, at a time when there were still wards with over 80 people, the first of many staff houses was turned over to use by 12 residents. This was followed by the division of wards. For example, a ward for 60 people became two wards with 30 people each. Later, wards were subdivided into four flats with up to five people in each. Throughout the 1970s staff became accustomed to the idea of domestic-scale living for residents and many gradually came to the conclusion that a hospital was not an appropriate place for them to live.

The early resettlement projects were all local, for small groups of two to four people in unstaffed group homes, with initiatives coming from Calderstones. The first took place in 1975 when four men were found a council house five miles away. This was stimulated by visits to Prestwich, a large psychiatric hospital in Salford, which had begun to develop group homes. Over the next few years several more people moved into ordinary houses within seven miles of Calderstones, including two women in their seventies. The received wisdom at the time was that it would be cruel to resettle elderly people who have lived many years in hospital. The experience of these two women showed that it would have been cruel to deny them the opportunity.

In 1979 a charge nurse set up home in what had been a staff house in the hospital grounds called Daisy Bank with two young deaf men and one of the profoundly handicapped adolescents from the ward where he worked. The model for this life-sharing arrangement came from L'Arche, which the charge nurse had visited (Wolfensberger 1973), and from the Cardiff University Social Services group home in which students shared a house with ex-residents of Ely Hospital (Mansell 1977). A year later the charge nurse moved back to his own home in Burnley with his profoundly handicapped young friend. The shared living arrangement at the hospital continued with another nurse until the two young men moved to their own house in Burnley.

During this time thinking was evolving. Leadership from the top was creating an expectation of change with initiatives which facilitated closer personal relationships between staff and residents. Tradition was being challenged. Before the publication of *An Ordinary Life* in 1980, there had been ten years of groundwork at Calderstones and some pioneering resettlement. *An Ordinary Life* clarified some issues and provided confirmation of the direction taken. More especially, it brought into the open the need for all concerned to examine some basic human values and decide where they stand on the right of people with learning disabilities to take their place as full members of the community.

In 1980 a resettlement team was created to bring together the people most actively concerned and give resettlement a focus. A resettlement officer was appointed to work full-time and the policy was established of a project team for each resettlement proposal. In 1981 a ward of ten children with profound learning disabilities together with the ward staff was relocated in two semi-detached houses in Nelson with five children in each. These were the first 24-hour staffed houses. Staff were outposted but continued to be managed from the hospital. It was immediately realised that five children per house was too many and this was later reduced to three per house. Other lessons were learned. No staff training had been given for the move and it was not possible to support staff as they had been in Calderstones. Some staff subsequently returned to the womb of the hospital. This project illustrates the commitment to learning how to do better from practical experience even in the face of great scepticism. A bias to action has been accompanied by a willingness to take risks. The first months were not easy. It took time for people in the neighbourhood to get used to having young people who behaved oddly in their midst.

Another of the children's wards moved in 1982 when a second young man went to live with the charge nurse in Burnley and two houses were rented from a housing association for a member of staff and two young people in each. The shared living approach grew out of the earlier experience at Daisy Bank. Slowly, the number of Calderstones people living in ordinary houses in Burnley, Pendle and Rossendale, the home catchment district, was increasing: 11 in 1982, 32 in 1984 and 55 by late 1986.

Most hospital staff have now come to terms with the idea of

resettlement. Over the years no staff could avoid the mass circulation in the hospital of published reports, national guidance and position papers emphasising community care and the philosophy of normalisation underpinning the policy. A strong in-service training department has been created and meetings, conferences, workshops and seminars at Calderstones have reiterated the theme. Extraordinary opportunities have been made available for attendance at similar events elsewhere. Many staff have come to support the 'ordinary life' idea vigorously; a very small number think it is totally misconceived. Surprisingly little opposition to resettlement has come from the unions, probably because of the extensive discussions that have taken place.

REGIONAL THINKING CHANGES

By the late 1970s, moves towards community living for people with learning disabilities were permeating a number of places around the North West. Nurses, psychologists, social workers and others were coming together in policy forums such as the Lancashire Area Health Authority Advisory Panel on Mental Handicap and the Regional Health Authority Mental Handicap Advisory Group.

In 1979 a regional plan was published for consultation which was seen by many people in the field as reactionary in seeking to perpetuate the traditional role of the hospitals. Because of the outcry the plan was shelved. Then in 1981 the regional health authority began to allocate money from revenue to district health authorities to develop community provision for people with learning disabilities. By 1983 this had built up to £5 million per year, mainly used to appoint staff.

In 1981, in preparation for the health service reorganisation of 1982, the Regional Mental Handicap Advisory Group was reconstituted, bringing together for the first time people who worked in learning disability services from around the region with staff from regional headquarters; this proved to be a most effective combination. As time went on the growing understanding and commitment of the four regional staff from planning, finance, nursing and medicine was essential in piloting the policy and its implementation at regional level. The task of the group was to formulate guidance for the district health authorities on how the new money should be spent. From the outset the group adopted a comprehensive approach, taking the view that no service for people with learning disabilities should be planned in isolation.

Members with a wide range of backgrounds in addition to health were sought, including social services, a voluntary body, the housing corporation, parents of a child with learning disability, education and later social security and the Manpower Services Commission. During 1982 there was extensive consultation on the draft policy *A Model District Service* (NWRHA 1983), which drew largely on the work of the now defunct Lancashire Area Health Authority. It was recognised that there had to be wide appreciation of the inter-relationships of each part of the overall system (see Ackoff 1980) if each agency and contributor was to cooperate in meeting the needs of people with learning disabilities.

Thoughtful design of the comprehensive local services advocated in *An Ordinary Life* became a matter for attention. Local staff sought an understanding of the principles of service design from program analysis of service systems (PASS) workshops. Three workshops on planning local services were held. These events helped to develop informal networks of people sharing common interests and values. Perhaps the single most important lesson that this story illustrates is that 'Dispersed but cohesive networks represent the strongest and most powerful infrastructure for both effective implementation of innovation and continued diffusion' (Emery 1982). Since early 1986, staff training has been enhanced by a regional training team of three people.

As the regional initiatives gathered pace, social services directors found that they needed to coordinate their efforts. The North West Association of Social Services Authorities came into being as well as a joint body of RHA and NWASSA members and officers to focus on issues arising from health and local authority developments across the North West.

The regional policy has concentrated on seeking ideals in order to provide the context and direction within which local services can work out details. Alternative directions, such as building-based services, have been firmly restricted in order that planning and development time should not be diverted from the task of enabling community living. The idea that some people with learning disabilities would always have to be segregated was still around. In order to further spell out the implications of community living for all service users outlined in *A Model District Service*, regional guidance was issued in 1985. *Services for People with Special Needs* (NWRHA 1985a) emphasised the need to explore community provision to the limit before segregative solutions are considered. *Implementing and Staffing a Model District Service* (NWRHA 1987) contributed further to the continuing dialogue on how local and comprehensive services can best be developed.

Having decided to provide clear leadership from region, various mechanisms are used to steer local developments in the direction of supporting community living. A regional development team was created in 1984 which can be invited in by district and local authorities to advise on service developments. The team consists of two part-time members who bring in people from around the region to help with visits. District reviews require that the annual plans of district health authorities are in line with regional policies. In addition, regional resources are released only for schemes which fit in with regional policy.

Gradually each district made a commitment to develop local services and promote community living and by 1984, the DHSS was encouraging the process of winding down long-stay hospitals in its regional reviews. The possibility of closing some of them was now on the agenda. Admissions of children had ceased and by 1985 all children had been relocated outside hospitals. A regional policy was adopted – *Rundown of Hospitals for People with Mental Handicap in the NW Region* (NWRHA 1985b) – and in 1986 a regional apppointment at a senior level was made to promote the relocation of services from those hospitals to the community.

Difficulties arose when the regional health authority's initiatives were misunderstood by some local authorities. However, adjustments have gradually been made, not least as a result of the requirement for health districts and local authorities to agree plans in order to receive regional funding. A funding policy was adopted in 1984 to facilitate the transfer of resources from hospital to the community (NWRHA 1984). Under the policy a sum of money becomes available to community services to provide for each person transferred from long-stay hospital to the community. The sum is based on the average cost of hospital provision for one resident (in 1986, £11,900 per annum).

The responsiveness of people and organisations to the rapid pace of change is illustrated by one local authority which found so much of its own business being taken up with matters arising from health service changes that it set up a weekly meeting specifically to deal speedily with these issues.

To assist local service providers in adapting as changes are implemented, a regional quality enhancement group has been set up. The search for high quality services requires constant review of what is happening to ensure that outcomes for service users are indeed improving.

LOCAL CHANGES

By late 1984 the move from hospital to community, now officially sanctioned by regional and district policies, was becoming more formalised in Burnley, Pendle and Rossendale. The houses which were still managed by the hospital were hived off to be managed by the newly created district mental handicap service. Nurse managers were appointed for each of the three localities.

In order to take stock of the situation, the health authority commissioned an evaluation of the process of resettlement by the Community and Mental Handicap Educational and Research Association (CMHERA) (Tyne and Williams 1984). The report on the evaluation gave recognition to the pioneering efforts and considerable progress made in improving the quality of life for people who had made the move to more ordinary living. However, some major challenges remain. How can people with learning disabilities participate more fully in the life of the community and develop relationships with non-handicapped people? How can the focus on people as individuals be maintained as the resettlement programme grows and the pressure to increase the rate of resettlement becomes greater? Coordination of the increased number of people and resources involved becomes an issue. Liaison with local services in all the catchment districts is in danger of becoming strained.

There is also a danger of conflict between health and local authorities. In catchment districts further away, much of the initiative for resettlement is being taken by social services departments. In Burnley, Pendle and Rossendale the initiative remains by agreement with the health service although a progressively greater shared approach is now developing between health and local authorities. Nurse managers have had to learn rapidly that transferring institutional management to a dispersed service creates problems concerning support to grassroots staff who have far more responsibility than when they were in a hospital ward.

A major difference between hospital and community services is that a change of staff in the community can have far greater disruptive effect. It appears that each staff member has greater impact in a dispersed service, both on service users and on other staff. Adjustment to a change of staff therefore can take much longer for all concerned. Another difference between hospital and community services is that support mechanisms for staff have to be more structured without the envelope of the institution.

CONDITIONS FOR EFFECTIVE CHANGE

If some clarity of direction and momentum for change in the North Western region has been achieved, why should this be so? There seems to have been a convergence of trends in the early 1980s which enabled large-scale changes to happen. The reorganisation of the health service in 1982 prompted the regional team of officers to commission guidance to help the newly created district health authorities take on their responsibilities for providing services for people with learning disabilities. Lancashire Area Health Authority, responsible up to that time for the region's three large mental handicap hospitals, had already done much of the thinking needed to bring its own policy up to date. In contrast to some other regions, the North Western Regional Health Authority was prepared to give firm central direction to its district health authorities. A coherent philosophy was becoming widely shared across the region through extensive PASS training.

There began to flourish a scattering of people in health and local authorities who learned how to make change happen by implementing local and comprehensive services. There was no strong medical presence defending institutional provision as in other parts of the country. Resources were not as constrained as elsewhere: the housing stock available to housing associations and local authorities is moderately plentiful and the region has gained from the redistribution of health service funds from the South East under RAWP.

CHALLENGES FOR THE FUTURE

Despite the high priority given to resettlement at national, regional, district and hospital levels, the so-called rush to the community has in fact only been a trickle. Large-scale changes have certainly happened. Much preparatory work has been done; attitudes have changed and many posts have been created in community services. It has been said that most of the more easily resettled people have now moved and that those still in hospital will require more support. A number of Calderstones residents regarded as challenges have been resettled. Currently a young man thought to be extremely difficult is being prepared, through the life-sharing arrangement, to move to his own house outside hospital. For many years he led a very restricted life because spasmodically he would strike out at anyone close enough.

For the past eight months he has been living in what was

previously a staff flat with a member of staff who works elsewhere in the hospital. Two other nurses work with him and the frequency of untoward incidents has dropped dramatically. He is now making his own way round the grounds of the hospital and has an individual programme in the hospital to keep him occupied.

Now that community living and resettlement from hospital has a much higher profile, some voices of dissent are being raised. Some older parents of residents in the long-stay hospitals have become anxious about the future of their sons and daughters. At a time of government funding cuts for both local authorities and hospital provision accompanied by government support for profit-making private proprietors, they fear there are inadequate quality safeguards both in hospital and in the community.

This is not the end of the story. Having got over the initial hump in moving away from segregative institutional provision, the priority is now to ensure that community services are truly comprehensive. Integration in education and employment have become the new frontiers. If individual rights are to be promoted and protected, citizen and collective advocacy schemes will be necessary (Wolfensberger 1977). Finally, we need to learn how to involve service users more fully in safeguarding 'an ordinary life'.

References

Ackoff R L (1980) The systems revolution. In: Lockett M and Spear R (eds). Organisations as systems. Milton Keynes, The Open University Press.

Emery M (1982) Searching for new directions, in new ways, for new times. Canberra, Centre for Continuing Education, Australian National University.

Mansell J (1977) (Student project at University College, Cardiff) Involvement of the client, the family and the community (Report of the Tenth Spring Conference on Mental Retardation). Exeter, National Society for Mentally Handicapped Children.

NWRHA (1983) Services for people with mental handicap: a model district service. Manchester, North Western Regional Health Authority.

NWRHA (1984) Mental handicap funding policy. Manchester, North Western Regional Health Authority.

NWRHA (1985a) Services for people with mental handicap: services for people with special needs. Manchester, North Western Regional Health Authority.

NWRHA (1985b) Rundown of hospitals for people with mental handicap in the NW Region. Manchester, North Western Regional Health Authority.

NWRHA (1987) Implementing and staffing a model district service. Manchester, North Western Regional Health Authority.

Tyne A and Williams P (1984) Evaluation by PASS of the relocation of people from Calderstones into ordinary housing in Burnley, Pendle and Rossendale. London, Community and Mental Handicap Educational and Research Association.

Wolfensberger W (1973) Overview of Jean Vanier and L'Arche. Toronto, National Institute on Mental Retardation.

Wolfensberger W (1977) A multi-component advocacy/protection schema. Toronto, National Institute on Mental Retardation.

Jim Mansell

Training for service development

In recent years extensive attempts have been made to clarify and disseminate ideas about the values on which services should be based and the forms they might take. The Community and Mental Handicap Educational and Research Association has used programme analysis of service systems (PASS) and programme analysis of service systems' implementation of normalisation goals (PASSING) workshops to disseminate the idea of normalisation (Wolfensberger and Glenn 1975; Wolfensberger 1980; Wolfensberger and Thomas 1983), and the King's Fund has done much to promote innovative models of residential and day services through workshops and publications in its 'an ordinary life' series (see Appendix I).

Government or local agencies may take the lead in adopting a clear philosophy of care and systematically promoting service development based on its tenets, but in many cases a lack of consensus prevents this. It may also be hard to distinguish lip-service (whether due to misunderstanding or for more cynical reasons) from real commitment before the process of service development is relatively advanced.

Within existing services there is little consensus about the aims of services or the effectiveness of different models. The policy of setting up community-based services may owe as much to pressure to sell valuable institutional sites as to any clear acceptance of a particular philosophy and set of responsibilities. Current policies in health authorities and social services departments have been formed reactively, reflecting a range of different pressures and demands and hampered by bargaining between professional groups. The result is an accretion of disparate and often contradictory strands, rather than any coherent statement of intent. Against this background, the severe shortage of resources makes people cautious about reaching towards the leading edge of service development. The long history of failure to achieve radical change in services for people with learning disabilities has produced a climate in many places in which only the most modest of improvements are attempted and anything more than marginal change is seen as unrealistic. In this sceptical, demoralised environment there may be no authoritative mandate for value-led change.

Thus, there will be many occasions in which there remains muddle and dispute about the future direction of services, with development paralysed by argument about the right direction to take. In this situation, the task of the trainer is to find a way of intervening in services which opens up the prospect for change. This entails both broadening the horizons of what is believed to be achievable, showing exemplary models of services, and helping people adopt approaches which lead them on to more ambitious goals as they achieve those set earlier. In broad terms, the aim is to contribute to the creation of services which have the potential for excellence and the organisational structures which have the capacity to strive for it. This is a rather wider remit than trainers often adopt, with major implications for the content and style of training.

UNDERSTANDING THE SERVICE DEVELOPMENT PROCESS

What is the most effective way of introducing new ideas from within the service agency, in the absence of a mandate for value-led change? Perhaps the most obvious approach would be to confront the people planning and running existing services with a direct challenge to clarify their values and the basis on which services should be organised. This would fit in well with the traditional rationalist approach to policy making. This approach emphasises the need to clarify in detail at the beginning the objectives the policy is to achieve and the nature of the interventions needed to achieve them. Implementation is then conceptualised as a simple process of replication, which often attracts less energy and interest than the initial debate.

Such an approach, however, has serious drawbacks. It requires that the alternative view held be regarded as authoritative. In so far as the radical view in services for people with learning disabilities remains a minority position held by a scattered and relatively powerless group, direct challenge might simply provoke the service agency to rule it out from the start and marginalise or exclude its proponents. And since, if the service is to strive for excellence, it needs to have a sense of ownership of the values and ideas involved, direct challenge may risk polarising views and reducing the ease with which new approaches can later be adopted. Thus, trying to win the argument in principle at the outset may not work. The alternative is to adopt a small-scale incrementalist approach, working with those in the service who do have good ideas to show new ways of doing things. In this way the training intervention, by demonstrating what can be achieved, can capture the imagination of less confident or committed planners who will then want to own a similar initiative. Thus, attempts to clarify and reinforce particular views or attitudes follow, rather than precede, involvement in new ways of working.

An iterative, incremental approach has another advantage: it allows radical development to start in advance of resolving the great philosophical debate. In doing so, it not only influences that debate more effectively than mere argument but ensures that the earliest start is made on providing decent services for people with learning disabilities where there is the greatest vision and commitment among service personnel. To do this requires a balance between the twin goals of coverage and excellence. Although the service agency must be concerned with coverage, so that minimum standards and expectations of fairness are satisfied, it is also an important part of the training function to help people achieve excellence, and this often means working with a smaller number of people to demonstrate success in relatively favourable conditions. Service managers are often most concerned about bringing all their services up to a minimally acceptable level; but it is the existence of excellent services which drives the process of service development by creating the tension between what could be and what is achieved.

This approach yields two ground rules for a training strategy. First, it means that most training effort needs to be directed towards showing by example rather than attempting to change the views of key decision makers directly. Second, the central concern has to be the development of excellent service projects with people who already have a clear vision of what they need to do, to serve as models to encourage others. Although there will still need to be a spread of training activity among services, it is important that training effort is not all taken up trying to bring basically unsound services above a minimum threshold.

TRAINING FOR SERVICE DEVELOPMENT

The paradox of staff training in relation to organisational performance is that while training is an intervention widely regarded as crucial to the successful achievement of the organisation's purposes, it is often ineffective in contributing towards this outcome. This is because training is usually too narrowly defined as improving the skills or attitudes of individuals outside the context of organisational change. Even if training does change individuals, there is no guarantee that their performance in the work setting will change: this may be due much more to lack of resources, lack of help or lack of encouragement than to individual skills or attitudes. A focus restricted to individuals may also reflect and reinforce an artificial separation of planning and management from the reality of work as experienced by front-line staff, so that staff and their trainers are blamed for failing to meet unrealistic or improper expectations generated elsewhere.

The effectiveness of services for people with learning disabilities is measured by the kind of *lifestyle* they enable individuals to have. Good services enable people, whatever their disabilities, to participate in a full range of household and community activities, to continue to develop their expertise and confidence (increasing the extent to which they direct their own lives) and to build up and maintain a network of supportive friendships and relationships. The lifestyle of people with learning disabilities is the product of a combination of individual and environmental factors: individual factors such as the imagination, skill and commitment of members of staff, and environmental factors such as the kind of services provided, the policies of the agency, the guidance available to staff, and the balance of incentives and motivation. To achieve effectiveness in services requires that these individual and organisational factors are tackled together in a consistent manner. Thus the role of the trainer extends into organisational development as a consultant to and trainer of the managers who define the environment in which staff work.

Another important characteristic of the environmental factors influencing service effectiveness is that some of them are defined in the planning of services, before front-line staff or the people they serve are present. Thus, the training intervention needs to start with the planning process and to encompass planners and managers as well as front-line staff. This is a natural extension of the principle involved in 'whole-establishment-training', which recognises the importance of working with the whole staff team and their managers (Whiffen 1984). A further component of this model is that, since effective services for people with learning disabilities will be characterised by good teamwork and coordination between different disciplines and service agencies, almost all training needs to take place in a multi-disciplinary and multi-agency context so that teamwork and coordination are high on the agenda and are practised through work on the training project.

This yields two more ground rules for training strategy. Training for the development of effective services involves working to make planning and management more responsive to issues in the lifestyle of the people served. It requires that every decision is made knowing its consequences for the consumers of the service, and implicitly it envisages that the needs of the individual people served will carry more weight than the procedures and policies which otherwise guide service design. This means that the trainer needs to work across traditional boundaries between planning, management and service delivery. And finally, training must be organised on a multi-disciplinary and multi-agency basis to preview the ways of working together which will be needed in new services.

Training for service development

1 Concentrate on showing by example rather than arguing philosophy in the abstract ('a bias for action').
2 Work mainly with people trying to develop innovative services ('back winners').
3 Bridge the planning and delivery of services to make planners and managers more responsive to the consequences of their decisions for the lifestyle of the people served (work with teams on real-life issues over relatively long periods).
4 Adopt a multi-disciplinary, multi-agency focus.

TRAINING IN THE ORGANISATION

The most important content area identified as a training need in the South East Thames Regional Health Authority in 1983 was the development of staffed housing for people with learning disabilities. Where they had any clear plans at all, most district health authorities envisaged providing residential care for people with severe or profound learning disabilities in various kinds of hostel or hospital setting. Involvement of the social services department in these plans was patchy and tentative. Only two districts (Medway and Lewisham) had firm plans for staffed housing.

133

The response to this need was a course called 'Developing staffed housing for mentally handicapped people'. This was open to applications from teams of people working locally to set up staffed housing; the teams had to be multi-agency, and access to places on the course was competitive. Each team had to commit two days every month or six weeks to attend the course, which ran from November 1983 to April 1985. Of the' 15 district health authorities in the region, 11 fielded teams of which all but one included both social and health service staff.

The course did not address the question of whether housing was the best form of residential option for people with learning disabilities, but started from the assumption that everyone attending was already committed to the 'ordinary life' model of care, at least on a pilot basis. Each workshop addressed the practical issues of thinking through the details of the project and how it would be implemented: the process of project definition, finding housing, obtaining planning permission, considering building design and equipment, staffing, training staff, and providing day care. Within each topic, the course included a) a framework for addressing the issues, derived from an early draft of a book (Mansell *et al* 1987), b) the experience of other projects or experts given in presentations, c) the opportunity for each local team to spend time on its own working out the details of its scheme and d) time for consultations between teams and advisers, either from the course team or from presenters. At every step in the development process, teams were challenged to consider the impact of their decisions on the lifestyle of the people served. Although important outcomes had to be compromised, teams were encouraged to adopt a developmental view in which each compromise was the best that could be achieved and with the knowledge of how it could be improved upon next time.

Evaluating the impact of training is always difficult and the more training is integrated into the process of service development the harder it is to untangle its own contribution. Other factors certainly influenced the development of staffed housing: the continuing pressure from national lobbies; the growth of mechanisms to make such developments easier; the example of the first schemes to come on stream. But it seems reasonable to credit the training intervention with some effect, both in terms of increasing the number of staffed housing schemes and in shifting the frame of consensus about acceptable kinds of service development at local level and in the regional health authority itself. By 1986, every district but one had at least some plans to include staffed housing in its provision.

Two other examples of this model of training intervention are being developed. The first is the development of services for people with severe learning disabilities who also have extremely challenging behaviour. Instead of building or refurbishing an institutional environment to replicate the containment service offered to these people until now, the regional health authority defined the objective as developing the local competence of services to provide a high quality service on the 'ordinary life' model. Once again, this means working with teams of local planners, managers and front-line staff to develop an individualised package of services (including a good home, meaningful day occupation and skilled help) for each of the relatively small number of individuals whose problems present a major challenge. The intervention here has been to set up a *special development team* (Emerson *et al* 1987) to undertake this advising, helping and progress-chasing role. The team's ability to promote high quality solutions is enhanced by having extra pump-priming funds it can make available to local services implementing agreed plans for named individuals. With a more explicit service development role, the special development team works closely with, but is separate from, the training team in the regional health authority.

The other main attempt to develop this model of work is in 'training the trainers' – developing the competence of local training staff to play their part in the development of local services for people with learning disabilities. At present local training is often fragmented and trainers feel unskilled and powerless to take the lead in advancing new ideas. The intervention is to carry out a *joint assessment of local training need* with representatives of the health authority, social services department and other local agencies to produce a contract for local and regional training initiatives. This will provide a clear mandate for a local multi-agency training team to work with regional staff over a two-year period. Part of this work comprises a *trainer's development programme*, including workshops on training methods and approaches to intervention in the services. This will also make use of specially developed video-assisted training materials in a series called 'Bringing people back home' (ESCATA/SETRHA 1987).

TRAINING INDIVIDUALS

The focus on organisational change helps create an environment receptive to innovation: there remains a desperate shortage of people to take up this challenge. High quality services require more staff than the poor quality options they replace, and the staff they need have to have more skill and confidence to achieve ambitious goals as well as the vision and commitment to identify them in the first place. Three distinct areas of training needs are immediately apparent: the basic training of qualified care staff (including staff in day or domiciliary services as well as in residential care), the post-qualification training of experienced care staff in meeting special needs and the post-qualification training of managers or aspiring managers who will form the cadre of leaders in the development of new services.

The major issue in the training of qualified care staff is the artificial obstacle of separate training for nurses and social services staff. Whatever the different strengths and weaknesses of the two professional groups in existing services (and both have easily identified strengths and weaknesses), it is clear that new services need staff who see themselves as one group of people able to work in a range of settings with people who have different levels of disability. Although arrangements for the joint operational management of services for people with learning disabilities at local level will help develop this team spirit, the obvious route to this goal is through increasing partnership in shared qualifying training.

In 1983 the district health authorities in East Sussex asked the regional health authority for help in setting up a shared qualifying training scheme. The regional health authority asked the Sussex Certificate in Social Service Scheme to convene a working party which soon reported that such a scheme was feasible and that the major obstacle was the attitude being taken at the time by the English National Board (ENB) and the Central Council for Education and Training in Social Work (CCETSW).

Over the following two years, extensive negotiation and consultation was undertaken with the validating bodies and in mid 1986 a joint committee of ENB and CCETSW indicated that the working party should proceed to implementation of a shared qualifying training scheme in January 1989, although this committee itself could not guarantee approval by the parent bodies. The working party has proceeded to prepare the scheme and has appointed a project officer. The regional health authority has continued to make strong representations nationally for the validating bodies to match the pace of service development in their thinking about validation. In 1985 a similar working party was set up between Bromley, Medway, Maidstone, and Tunbridge Wells health authorities and the Bromley Certificate in Social Service Scheme and its associated social services departments.

This too has appointed a project officer to prepare a local scheme for shared qualifying training.

Until these schemes are operational, new services have to rely on staff with traditional qualifications (like the Certificate in Social Service or Registered Nurse of the Mentally Handicapped) or on recruiting people with unorthodox or no formal qualifications. This places a heavy load on the induction training required locally to re-orient staff to the new model of care, particularly for staff from hospital or hostel services who will rely on the induction training in the new service for the main part of their retraining needs (since it is not feasible to create the model of care needed to retrain in the old services). It will also cause problems later in the career development of staff the service needs to retain but who lack widely recognised formal qualifications.

Meanwhile, the National Health Service Training Authority has funded a five-year project to develop a model of post-qualification training for experienced care staff working with people who have special needs. This has just started and will initially involve work with staff in new services to identify what would constitute exemplary performance in the areas of most concern. It is already clear that one major area is in helping front-line staff in positions of leadership to develop hands-on skills in the application of behaviour analysis methods within the framework of the principle of normalisation. Qualifying training can do no more than give a general introduction to these issues and clinical psychologists are often too rare and too little involved in hands-on work to make much impact; yet many people with learning disabilities have special needs which require the imaginative and principled application of powerful instructional technologies in a consistent way over very long periods. Failure to provide staff with the skills to deliver sufficiently intense and relevant individual programmes generates very high levels of anxiety for staff and the people they serve, and may lead to burn-out among the former and to victim-blaming and exclusion for the latter.

Finally, a management development programme has been started in the form of an MA in Applied Psychology of Mental Handicap Services at the University of Kent at Canterbury. This offers 10 five-day workshops over two years linked with practical work in the manager's own agency, and is designed to produce the cadre of managers who will lead the development of community-based services for people with learning disabilities. The programme is open to managers from a wide range of backgrounds and the first people accepted represent a spread of agencies and professions. The central aim of the course is to integrate the organisational and individual perspectives in developing and running services. The practical work includes both a project to track the experience of an individual with learning disabilities receiving services and a service development project designed to plan, introduce and evaluate some aspect of innovative practice in the manager's own service. Thus each manager will gain experience of applying the approaches discussed in a real work situation and the agency will benefit from the innovation itself and from the experience of adjusting to innovation as it happens.

RENEWAL

Thus far the main emphasis of the training interventions described has been on developing new models of service. In the early stages of development, high levels of enthusiasm and commitment among the people taking the lead do much to sustain the vision of what the new services should aim to achieve. But the experience of other innovations in services for people with learning disabilities shows that this initial enthusiasm will ebb away under the many pressures of implementation. There is, therefore, a need to build in safeguards against the decay of idealism and the trend for new services to slip back into the practices of the past.

In this too, training blends imperceptibly with the way services are organised. The training need is to help staff build decision-making structures that are sensitive and responsive to the needs and preferences of individual people with learning disabilities and which foster the process of reaching for more ambitious goals and working hard to achieve them. It is this process – understanding how management can make quality matter for front-line staff – which is at the heart of safeguarding services, rather than monitoring against minimum standards with the punitive, defensive climate this often entails.

This kind of training is now planned in two projects funded with the support of the National Health Service Training Authority. The first addresses the relationship between teams of front-line staff in houses and day services and their managers, drawing on models of participative management to create a climate in which staff are empowered to improve the service they offer. This is likely to start with a pilot project involving five or six teams of keen participants who will develop the approach before including others who wish to join in. The second project deals with the development of shared perspectives and approaches across health, social services and private and voluntary agencies. This will focus on the dimensions of service quality different agencies respond to, the different levels of achievement they are prepared to accept on each dimension, the different sources of evidence they use and the different steps they take to achieve improvements. The aim is not to impose uniformity but to understand the reasons for diversity and develop a training package which allows managers to draw their approaches together more consistently.

Work is also under way to consolidate the use of training in the principle of normalisation. PASS workshops have been used to provide individuals with a basic introduction simply to 'seed' existing services with people who understand the ideas involved. A need is now being identified to support people who have already attended introductory workshops but need help to introduce new ideas in their services. PASS or the new 'Five accomplishments' workshop (O'Brien 1987) are also likely to play a larger part in assessing service quality where monitoring is required.

Finally, the host organisation itself needs to invest in renewal and to reconsider the philosophy on which it bases its service development, the achievements it has made, the compromises it has succumbed to and the weaknesses and failures which remain. Senior officers of service agencies are denied almost any time in which to reflect on these issues: they are driven by the tasks of the moment just as front-line staff are often driven by the demands of the daily routine. This means that ideas move ahead faster than policies can keep up, and there is a need every few years for a re-statement of the overall mission of services and the broad framework of ideas within which development should now proceed. This should lead to the production of a revised policy addressing the quality goals of services. This policy should include some limits on which service models are no longer considered acceptable as new developments and should define what are the new 'boundaries of the possible' to which people should aspire.

Acknowledgments

The author would like to acknowledge the contribution of Peter Wakeford, Hilary Brown, Peter McGill, Eric Emerson, Sandra Hoskin and Peter Lindley in developing the work described here. More details of the specific training interventions under way in South East Thames Regional Health Authority are contained in a series of reports available from Jim Mansell at the Institute of Social and Applied Psychology, University of Kent at Canterbury.

References

ESCATA and South East Thames Regional Health Authority (1987) Bringing people back home: six video-assisted training packages. Brighton, ESCATA.

Emerson E, Barratt S, Bell C, Cummings R, McCool C, Toogood A and Mansell J (1987) Developing services for people with severe learning difficulties and challenging behaviours. Canterbury, University of Kent Institute of Social and Applied Psychology.

Mansell J, Felce D, Jenkins J, de Kock U and Toogood S (1987) Developing staffed housing for people with mental handicaps. Tunbridge Wells, Costello.

O'Brien J (1987) A guide to personal futures planning. In: Bellamy G T and Wilcox B (eds). A comprehensive guide to the activities catalog: an alternative curriculum for youth and adults with severe disabilities. Baltimore, Paul H Brookes.

Whiffen P (1984) Initiatives in in-service training: helping staff to care for mentally handicapped people in the community (paper 5.2). London, Central Council for Education and Training in Social Work.

Wolfensberger W (1980) The definition of normalisation: update, problems, disagreements and misunderstandings. In: Flynn R J and Nitsch K E (eds). Normalisation, social integration and community services. Baltimore, University Park Press.

Wolfensberger W and Glenn L (1975) Programme analysis of service systems. Toronto, National Institute on Mental Retardation.

Wolfensberger W and Thomas S (1983) PASSING: programme analysis of service systems' implementation of normalisation goals. Toronto, National Institute on mental Retardation.

David Towell

Managing strategic change

The preceding chapters report some of the extensive efforts around the country in the last eight years to enhance the opportunities available to people with learning disabilities; they also provide evidence of the real benefits in people's lives where these efforts have been successful. As Ann Shearer observes in *Building Community* (1986), 'there are all sorts of people in all sorts of places who have the ideas that make for change, and all sorts of people who help them to make it happen'.

This commitment to widespread participation in seeking improvements has been an important strength of the 'an ordinary life' initiative. The developments described in Part Two show that leadership can come from many quarters and that effective change is likely to involve mobilising coalitions of the key stakeholders in existing services.

However, as Shearer continues, 'the real challenge is to seek [the people with ideas for change] out, provide the structures which encourage them – and weld their efforts into a whole which can truly be called a comprehensive local service, available to anyone with a mental handicap, whatever their needs'.

It is this challenge of achieving comprehensive local services and doing so on a large scale which provides the focus for this chapter. While continuing to stress the importance of widespread participation in change, I shall be addressing particularly the people with formal leadership responsibilities – the members and senior managers of relevant public and voluntary agencies, and the officers (particularly in the NHS and local authorities) engaged in implementation.

The chapter is organised around four main themes. David King (1986) has recently argued that nothing is of greater strategic importance (to the NHS) than the 'care in the community concept'. Drawing on my own work, particularly with agencies in the South West of England, I begin by exploring the nature of this policy as it affects public services and identifying why it should be regarded as requiring *strategic* change.

This analysis suggests the relevance of the recent literature on strategic management and leads to my second theme – the importance for senior managers of considering the relevant environmental *context* and organisational *processes* as well as the *content* of new services in planning change. In particular I shall argue that success in implementing new patterns of services is only likely to be achieved where attention to the *substance* of 'an ordinary life' is complemented by adequate investment in developing the *capacity* of public agencies to establish and maintain high quality provision. This implies a leadership prepared to balance the concentration on relatively short-term tasks (fostered by existing planning systems and accountability reviews) with a real concern for building organisational effectiveness, developing appropriate processes of planning and management, training staff and creating an organisational culture which encourages informed innovation.

Recognising that we are still only at an early stage in achieving the transition to comprehensive community-based services, these arguments lead in turn to my third theme – the importance to success in managing change of *organisational learning* (that is, systematic efforts to improve agency performance by reviewing progress and pooling experience – see Argyris and Schon 1978). Roger Blunden in Chapter 9 stresses that service development is necessarily a dynamic process and the case studies of change in both the North West (Chapter 10) and South East Thames regions (Chapter 11) illustrate well the commitment there to learning from experience as implementation proceeds. Building on my second theme, I shall be suggesting that this attention to learning should be concerned with both the substance of change (the impact of services on their users) and the processes of change (how the strategy is being defined and implemented). These themes are developed more concretely through discussing the component elements of a major strategy for change and describing some of the mechanisms which have been established to foster learning in the South West.

Finally, I summarise the implications of these arguments for my fourth theme – the *leadership behaviour* required for managing strategic change. I shall be emphasising the importance of policy makers and senior managers themselves demonstrating commitment to a new vision of the opportunities which services should make available to people with learning disabilities while at the same time enabling operational staff to use their initiative in implementing this vision.

THE STRATEGIC CHALLENGE

There are several reasons why the transition towards community-based patterns of services should be regarded as strategically significant for public agencies. Recent years have been marked by two complementary trends: increasing recognition of the importance of planning local services on the basis of explicit principles and the flowering of innovative services which aim to demonstrate these principles in practice. As I noted in the introduction to this book, partly because of these trends the current context is one in which incremental growth is being overtaken by pressures for more rapid change, particularly associated with deinstitutionalisation in the NHS. The 'care in the community' arrangements in England and the 'all Wales strategy' have offered new financial incentives for movement. Within the NHS at least, government is pushing regional health authorities towards bold plans. The South Western RHA, for example, is publicly committed to developing new patterns of local services which will make all its institutions redundant within the next seven years.

As Ann Shearer (1986) shows, many of the good services we already have are partial, small-scale and well-resourced, at least in the energy and quality of leadership involved in their creation. These more radical strategies now pose the qualitatively different challenge of reproducing comprehensive local services on a *large scale* and in typical settings, within a wider financial and political climate which is far from supportive.

The implementation of these strategies has major organisational implications. Change involves a shift in the *location* of services – away from centralised, institutional provision towards dispersed, community-based services. In many places (including the South West) it involves also a shift in *agency responsibilities* – away from the NHS towards a coordinated pattern of multi-agency services in which local authorities have the main responsibility for ensuring integrated residential and day provision for everyone in their area.

More fundamentally, these organisational changes are of course intended to contribute to considerable improvements in the *quality* of services as reflected in the lives of people with learning disabilities and their families: a shift away from segregated, ineffective and devaluing provision towards new services which provide opportunities and support for everyone to lead as normal a life as possible in the community.

143

These substantive changes in services cannot be achieved on a large scale without significant innovations in the *ways* public services work. As Williams and Tyne argue in Chapter 1, new patterns of provision should not be static. Even the best of current services have weaknesses, for example in the extent of client participation in activities with non-disabled people. One requirement, therefore, is to find ways of building into local services the capacity for dynamic evolution and quality assurance.

As Williams and Tyne also argue from their PASS-based evaluations, planning, management and staff support arrangements are all typically poor in the emerging services, leaving many fragile and vulnerable. Another requirement, therefore, is to develop more appropriate and sensitive management systems. More subtly, community-based services entail a new relationship between public agencies and the people served: a move away from the tradition of 'providers and receivers' towards a model in which paid staff, people with learning disabilities and the general public are all active participants in creating more integrated communities. There is thus also a requirement for greater decentralisation in decision making – to bring together different agency contributions close to the consumers – and for a shift in organisational culture – from paternalism towards partnership.

There is considerable evidence that the magnitude of these challenges is typically being underestimated. As the House of Commons Social Services Committee (1985) argued persuasively, current opportunities for worthwhile change may therefore be wasted. One danger is that through concentrating on only some of these strategic issues the process of change will be distorted. Korman and Glennerster (1985) show, for example, that without adequate attention to the principles underpinning service development, it is possible to move people and resources without greatly improving the quality of new provision. Another danger is that the priority being given to deinstitutionalisation – while desirable in itself – will put the NHS in the driving seat for reform: this may undermine the inter-agency collaboration required to develop comprehensive local services which address unmet needs within the community as well as those of existing hospital residents. A further danger is that radical aspirations will be pursued without adequate attention to the organisational structures and processes required to implement – and sustain – the new forms of provision.

ELEMENTS IN STRATEGIES FOR PRINCIPLED CHANGE

How can these challenges be tackled? The recent literature on strategic management (for example, Parston 1986) offers a variety of insights drawn from the experiences of large organisations undergoing major upheavals. Particularly helpful is the framework developed by my late colleague Tom Evans. He argues (Evans 1986) that strategic management requires a continuous cycle of diagnosis, development and review: diagnosis of the strengths and weaknesses of the organisation in the light of the opportunities and problems it faces; development of the organisation's substantive activities and organisational capabilities in response to this diagnosis; and review as elements of the diagnosis and response change. More specifically, *strategy* involves coordinating a number of different strands of activity relating to:

- substantive strategy (the vision of future services, principles for assessing quality, the content of plans for moving forward);
- environmental relationships (building support, developing opportunities, addressing constraints and coping with external uncertainties in pursuing service objectives);
- resource allocation (mobilising appropriate sources of revenue, formulating financial policies which promote the substantive strategy);
- organisational development (establishing the planning and management arrangements, the structures and systems, required to implement and sustain new patterns of services);
- personnel development (improving managerial capacity, fostering staff commitment, training people for new roles);
- cultural change (promoting shared values and beliefs, building adaptability).

These aspects of strategy have implications throughout the organisation and Evans (1983) stresses the importance of implementation managers as essential mediators (in both directions) between broad strategy and the operational work of developing and delivering services.

In the case of large-scale strategies for developing community-based services for people with learning disabilities, the 'organisation' is in fact a multi-agency *system*. In the South West, the regional health authority, five county councils and eleven district health authorities are centrally involved (themselves internally subdivided, for example, into county council departments) together with other public agencies and voluntary associations. Developing a coherent strategy requires a wide variety of activities at different levels and in different parts of this total system.

Applying ideas on strategic management to experiences in the South West and other similar situations, it has proved useful as a first approximation to distinguish three dimensions of concerted strategies for change:

— establishing the strategic framework
— designing and developing community-based services
— managing existing centralised services, particularly the contracting institutions.

Figure 3 illustrates the interdependence of the three dimensions and identifies key issues which need to be addressed. Reflection on these experiences suggests sixteen general requirements in achieving change. (The precise implications of these requirements will of course vary according to the situation and state of progress in different places.)

THROUGHOUT THE SYSTEM:

1 *The development of new services should be based on explicit values and a positive vision of the opportunities which should be available to people with learning disabilities.* Both to overcome the weaknesses of existing services and to energise the movement for reform, it is vital (as Chapter 1 argues more fully) that change should be informed by explicit principles which make clear how new services are intended to enhance the life experiences of people with learning disabilities. For the main agencies involved this means working for a commitment to comprehensive local services whose quality is judged by their effectiveness (see Chapter 9) in promoting the presence and participation of people with learning disabilities in the community.

2 *Comprehensive and effective local services can only be planned and delivered through real collaboration between the NHS, local authorities and other relevant agencies.* Community-based services which provide this wide range of opportunities and support to people with learning disabilities over the life cycle must draw on contributions from several public agencies, including local authority education, housing, social services and leisure departments, the NHS, employment services and social security offices, as well as from voluntary agencies. There are typically differences of interest, of professional perspective and

146

Figure 3   Key issues in concerted strategies for change

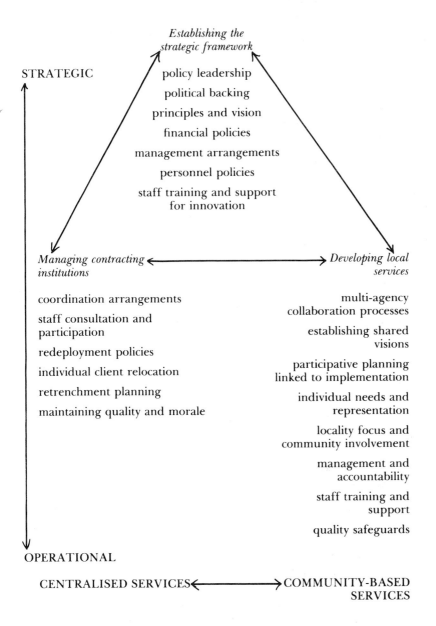

STRATEGIC

Establishing the
strategic framework

policy leadership

political backing

principles and vision

financial policies

management arrangements

personnel policies

staff training and support
for innovation

Managing contracting
institutions

Developing local
services

coordination arrangements

staff consultation and
participation

redeployment policies

individual client relocation

retrenchment planning

maintaining quality and morale

multi-agency
collaboration processes

establishing shared
visions

participative planning
linked to implementation

individual needs and
representation

locality focus and
community involvement

management and
accountability

staff training and
support

quality safeguards

OPERATIONAL

CENTRALISED SERVICES ←————→ COMMUNITY-BASED
SERVICES

147

mismatches of organisation between these agencies; in the past services have often been fragmented. It is essential, however (see for example Chapters 3 and 4), that members, managers and providers develop appropriate methods at different levels for working together in the interests of people with learning disabilities and their families.

3 *Region-wide initiative needs to be complemented by strong local leadership and widespread participation in achieving change.* While impetus from strategic authorities (for example, the regional health authority) is important in stimulating and sustaining the momentum for change, particularly in situations where service development problems cut across local administrative boundaries, new patterns of services cannot be achieved by 'top-down' planning and hierarchical control. Rather, real changes in services at the point where people with learning disabilities and direct providers meet require strong local leadership and local commitment. The region-wide contribution should therefore be concerned with establishing a broad strategic framework which fosters, supports and learns from purposeful local action. Large-scale change depends on the variety and vigour of small-scale initiatives.

ESTABLISHING THE STRATEGIC FRAMEWORK:

4 *A region-wide strategic framework should be developed to provide leadership on policies relating to the direction and rate of change; resource allocation; planning and management arrangements; manpower development; and support for innovation.* It follows from the preceding points that regional health authorities need to negotiate with local authorities and other relevant agencies a regionwide joint approach to key strategic issues, always in support of local service development tailored to meet local needs. Among the issues this framework should address are the rate of movement towards community-based services and the planning and management arrangements required to coordinate change. Also important are the personnel and training policies needed to foster staff commitment and ensure that appropriately skilled people are available to provide new services. In addition, regional arrangements will be required to monitor progress, evaluate significant developments and provide assistance to local problem-solving.

5 *This framework should include financial policies which recognise that*

extra resources are required to provide good community-based services and that dispersed services should mobilise dispersed sources of revenue. The substantial assets of money and skill tied up in traditional services can be used more effectively in providing community-based services. However, given the poor quality of much existing provision, the total public sector cost of new services which aspire to comprehensiveness is likely to be significantly greater than current expenditure. During the transition period there is also a need for 'bridging' finance to provide incentives for local innovation while protecting standards in existing services. Meeting these needs is likely to require financial policies which increase the NHS and local authority investment in services for people with learning disabilities while mobilising other resources, for example, from the Manpower Services Commission, housing associations and the contributions of people themselves (from earnings and DHSS benefits).

6 *Radical strategies require continuing efforts to build and sustain political support in the context of changing external pressures.* In the past, services for people with learning disabilities have not been given consistent priority in the contest with more 'popular' causes (for example, acute medical specialties within the NHS). Important stakeholders in existing services may be ambivalent about change. The main agencies may be faced with new demands and unexpected external pressures. Given the magnitude and duration of the transition towards local services, it follows that progress is only likely to be maintained where efforts are made to build political support for reform – expressed, for example, in the commitment of authority members and the interest of community representatives as well as in advocacy by internal coalitions.

DEVELOPING COMMUNITY-BASED SERVICES:

7 *At local level the processes for multi-agency planning should themselves be carefully designed to ensure widespread participation and strong links with implementation.* New patterns of local services can only be created where traditional bureaucratic approaches to planning and implementation are replaced by a more organic process of service development – characterised both by coherent leadership and widespread participation in achieving change on the basis of explicit principles. It is at local level

that all the legitimate interests can be engaged in the debate necessary both to shape and gain commitment to a new vision of future provision, starting from the experiences and aspirations of people with learning disabilities. Service design then involves exploring alternative modes of provision (drawn from experience elsewhere and local invention – see Part Two) in order to identify how best to meet individual needs according to the agreed principles. As part of these processes, involvement of people directly engaged in service delivery, attention to how favoured ideas can be translated into practice and review of subsequent action are all required to ensure that planning and implementation are fully integrated.

8 *Services should be planned to meet individual needs and wishes.* In the past, particularly where planning has addressed the requirements of large populations, the needs of people with learning disabilities have been aggregated into ill-defined categories which fail to reflect individual diversity. There has also been a tendency to concentrate on people's disabilities rather than their abilities and to define needs in terms of the way services are currently provided rather than functionally, by the assistance actually required. The new approach to planning should begin instead from a careful assessment of individual strengths, needs and wishes and aim to deliver services which meet changing individual requirements (as expressed, for example, in individual programme plans – see Chapter 4). Planning for comprehensive services should address the needs both of people with learning disabilities living locally and those returning from institutional settings.

9 *Service development should therefore involve people with learning disabilities themselves.* It follows that local planning must involve people with learning disabilities themselves, supported by independent sources of advice and representation to strengthen their voice in service development. (A wide variety of methods to promote user participation are discussed in Chapter 2.)

10 *Service development should also seek to foster partnership between community services and the community itself.* The development of genuinely community-based services and a wide range of opportunities for people with learning disabilities cannot be achieved solely by welfare agencies and their paid employees. Rather, the participative approach to planning must seek to foster partnership between community services and the

community itself, both to gain public support for new patterns of local services and, more significantly, to promote fuller integration of people with learning disabilities in ordinary community life (see Chapter 5).

11 *Both the development and delivery of community-based services require an emphasis on locality as the focus for comprehensive provision.* Assessing individual needs, developing services which are responsive to local differences (for example, in social class and ethnicity), working with generic community services and building this partnership are all easier to achieve where planning for the populations of large administrative areas (health districts, boroughs and so on) starts by addressing the requirements of people in small localities (with populations of perhaps 20,000–30,000). Integrated delivery of comprehensive local services is also likely to depend on relevant agencies decentralising operational management to the locality level.

12 *Organisational arrangements and management processes should be carefully designed to ensure effective service coordination and explicit accountability for the tasks involved in service delivery.* These features of service development should of course be reflected in the continuing arrangements for organising and managing services established by relevant agencies. It is particularly important that decentralised management and widespread participation are combined with clear role definitions and accountability arrangements. Service designs should include explicit operational policies, job descriptions and staff procedures – all tied to the intended outcomes for users and reviewed regularly in the light of experience.

13 *New ways of working and new patterns of delivery require a significant investment in staff training and support.* It follows from the preceding points that managers and other staff will require a wide range of training opportunities (see Chapter 11) in order to explore the values, acquire the knowledge and develop the skills required to plan, implement and deliver high quality services. There will also be a need for support arrangements which help to maintain staff commitment and promote effective problem-solving.

14 *Local services should build in safeguards for quality.* If local services are to learn from experience, correct mistakes and avoid drifting away from their initial objectives, it is important that specific mechanisms for reviewing progress and assuring

quality are established (see Chapter 9). These mechanisms should include external safeguards provided, for example, through the involvement of user representatives and independent evaluation studies.

MANAGING EXISTING CENTRALISED SERVICES:

15 *Existing centralised services should be closely linked with the development of community-based alternatives.* Strategic change has major implications for existing centralised services, notably the large institutions but also, for example, special schools and adult training centres. It is important that institutional concerns are neither dominant nor excluded from the development of alternatives. Rather these services should be represented with other groups in local planning processes and operational management should include clear arrangements for coordinating change (for example, the relocation of institutional residents) across the boundaries between old and new services.

16 *Existing centralised services require positive management during change to maintain standards and encourage staff support for change.* At the same time it is vital to recognise that management of existing centralised services during a lengthy period of transformation is itself a major task. The large hospitals in particular require high quality management committed to involving staff in maintaining and where possible improving standards while relocation is proceeding. From the outset this should include the negotiation of personnel and training policies which seek to maximise continuity of employment and prepare staff for movement into new services.

LEARNING HOW TO DO BETTER

Taken together these sixteen requirements for achieving strategic change present an enormous challenge. Nowhere yet in Britain has this challenge been tackled successfully. It would be unrealistic therefore to expect to get all these things 'right' together. Rather, in the South West and elsewhere managers are always likely to be in the position of *working towards* more effective strategies for developing and maintaining high quality community-based services. This requires careful judgments about where to put most effort at different stages in lengthy programmes of change. It also requires a strong investment in learning how to do better: learning how to improve services (as measured by their impact on the lives of people with learning disabilities) and learning how to improve the organisation's capabilities so that the prospects for successful service development are maximised. In managerial climates where certitude is taken as a sign of competence or where presentation is mistaken for performance, it may also require learning how to learn.

How can organisational learning be promoted? A starting point must be in managerial attitudes which appreciate the importance of learning both from successes and from mistakes. Reflecting on achievements and sharing the lessons with others can be potent methods for encouraging collective progress. Equally, as John O'Brien (1987) has recently argued, there is a great deal to be learnt by embracing ignorance, error and fallibility: by being 'thoughtful and decisive about what we don't know; what goes wrong as we act on our commitments; and where the limits to our abilities are'.

Given these attitudes there are significant opportunities for learning from existing management mechanisms but there is also likely to be a need to enhance the capacity for organisational learning by developing new methods (Towell 1981).

In the South West, for example, it is recognised that the impetus for high quality services must be developed locally within a broad strategic framework which provides the parameters for change. Within this context the regional health authority, in collaboration with county council representatives, has a variety of mechanisms available to review progress across the region. Both authority members and top managers get together on occasions to share views. Within the NHS, the planning system provides a formal vehicle for interaction between the regional health authority and district health authorities about the content and financing of local plans. An annual programme of region/district reviews promotes dialogue about progress and prospects. There are also more informal opportunities for officers with particular general management briefs (finance, manpower and so on) to explore relevant policy issues.

In addition, the agencies involved in this strategy have created a number of supplementary methods for learning from experience across the region, centred on two main vehicles: the *workshop* for officers leading the process of implementation and the *strategy support unit* (SWRHA 1985, 1986, 1987). The workshop brings together regional health authority officers and the representatives of other relevant agencies with implementation managers from each of the health and local authorities. It provides opportunities for exchanging information on local progress and problems, developing 'mutual aid' initiatives designed to improve performance and reviewing region-wide policies in the light of their local impact.

The strategy support unit (a multi-professional group of staff from different parts of the region led jointly by a chief officer from the regional health authority and a social services director representing his colleagues) is a method for pursuing these workshop objectives continuously. Its members provide the core of small 'peer review' teams (also including officers with other local experience) which visit each district/local authority to assist managers and professional staff in assessing progress. It coordinates working groups set up to develop and test better ways of addressing particular problems (for example, the design of community-based services for people with very challenging behaviour – see Chapter 8). It promotes relevant training initiatives. And on the basis of these activities, it offers advice both 'upwards' (to the strategic authorities) and 'downwards' (to local services) on ways of strengthening the prospects for success.

Within local agencies a similar range of initiatives is emerging. Among existing mechanisms, managerial reviews, joint training activities and individual programme planning are being used to encourage reflection and foster fresh ideas on operational issues. In addition, new planning methods (search conferences, 'getting to know you' exercises), development of quality assurance procedures, strengthening of user participation and selective evaluation studies are all widening opportunities for learning.

IMPLICATIONS FOR LEADERSHIP

The preceding analysis has impressive implications for the role of leadership in achieving large-scale change (see also Pettigrew 1986) and for the orientations and skills required of people with formal leadership responsibilities.

In summary and expressed ideally, five main leadership functions have been identified. First and foremost, leadership is required to orchestrate the new vision of future services and promulgate clear messages about the rationale and objectives for change throughout the system. Leaders will need to demonstrate through their own behaviour their commitment to the principles of *An Ordinary Life* and their dominant concern with the impact of decisions at all levels on the lives of people with learning disabilities.

Second, leadership is about gaining and maintaining support for the implementation of this vision. Looking 'upwards' and 'outwards' it is about building an authoritative mandate for change and mobilising political commitment to making the necessary resources available. It is about coping too with environmental pressures and uncertainties in ways which keep a clear sense of direction within the organisation. Internally, it is also about building widespread support while accepting doubts, encouraging constructive debate and providing assistance to people in working through the conflicts involved in achieving change.

Third, effective leadership needs to be based on the premise that successful development and delivery of high quality services requires a wide variety of action at different levels and in different parts of the multi-agency system, particularly of course at 'street level' where providers and people with learning disabilities meet. Leadership has therefore an important function in organisational development – creating and protecting the conditions which enable and support the operational work of subordinate staff. Leadership is also required to ensure that a complex mission is broken down into specific objectives and short-term action plans which structure and integrate the efforts of a wide range of people.

Fourth, leadership is about making change 'stick'. Innovation is rarely achieved once and for all: it has to be maintained over time in the face of the many pressures which can undermine the original goals and be renewed continually in the light of fresh ideas and opportunities. Leadership is required to ensure that new ways of organising and delivering services are supported by the wider policies and procedures of the public agencies involved. It is also important in establishing explicit forms of accountability for performance and appropriate quality assurance arrangements.

Fifth, leadership has a critical role in developing the commitment and capacity for organisational learning. Leadership is required which maintains an overview of progress towards strategic objectives, identifying unanticipated consequences of good intentions and enabling mid-course corrections to be made. It involves encouraging opportunities for sharing successes and learning from what is being attempted elsewhere. Finally, leadership involves promoting a culture in which people face up honestly to the limitations in what is currently being achieved for and with people with learning disabilities and support each other in the continuing struggle to do better.

Acknowledgments

Much of this analysis draws on work in the South West of England financially supported by the South Western Regional Health Authority. I am grateful to a large number of people in the South West for the opportunity to share ideas and experiences. I am also particularly indebted to John Rimmer who provided detailed comments on an earlier version of this chapter from his own observations in Australia, the United States and Britain.

References

Argyris C and Schon D A (1978) Organizational learning: a theory of action perspective. Reading, Massachusetts, Addison Wesley.

Evans T (1983) The unit manager. In: Wickings I (ed). Effective unit management. London, King Edward's Hospital Fund for London.

Evans T (1986) Strategic response to environmental turbulence. In: Parston G (ed). Managers as strategists: health services managers reflecting on practice. London, King Edward's Hospital Fund for London.

House of Commons (1985) Community care with special reference to adult mentally ill and mentally handicapped people. Second report from the Social Services Committee, session 1984–5, Volume I. London, HMSO.

King D (1986) The local dimension: care in the community. In: Parston G (ed). Managers as strategists: health services managers reflecting on practice. London, King Edward's Hospital Fund for London.

Korman N and Glennerster H (1985) Closing a hospital: the Darenth Park project. London, Bedford Square Press.

O'Brien J (1987) Embracing ignorance, error and fallibility: competencies for leadership of effective services. In: Taylor S (ed). Community integration. New York, Teachers College Press of Columbia University.

Parston G (ed) (1986) Managers as strategists: health services managers reflecting on practice. London, King Edward's Hospital Fund for London.

Pettigrew A M (1986) Managing strategic change. In: Parston G (ed). *op cit.*

Shearer A (1986) Building community with people with mental handicaps, their families and friends. London, Campaign for

People with Mental Handicaps and King Edward's Hospital Fund for London.

SWRHA (1985) Developing community-based services for people with mental handicap in the South West. Bristol, South Western Regional Health Authority.

SWRHA (1986) Achieving high quality community-based services for people with learning disabilities in the South West. Bristol, South Western Regional Health Authority.

SWRHA (1987) Maintaining momentum in developing high quality community-based services for people with mental handicap in the South West. Bristol, South Western Regional Health Authority.

Towell D (1981) Developing better services for the mentally ill: an exploration of learning and change in complex agency networks. In: Barrett S and Fudge C (eds). Policy and action. London, Methuen.

Publications in the 'An ordinary life' series

Published by King Edward's Hospital Fund for London

Fundamentals of service design

King's Fund (1982) An ordinary life: comprehensive locally-based residential services for mentally handicapped people (project paper 24, 2nd edition).

King's Fund (1984) An ordinary working life: vocational services for people with mental handicap (project paper 50).

Shearer A (1986) Building community with people with mental handicaps, their families and friends. (Published jointly with Campaign for People with Mental Handicaps.)

Blunden R and Allen D (eds) (1987) Facing the challenge: an ordinary life for people with learning difficulties and challenging behaviour.

King's Fund (forthcoming) An ordinary community life.

Supporting Papers

Shearer A (1981) Bringing mentally handicapped children out of hospital (project paper 30).

Heron A (1982) Better services for the mentally handicapped? Lessons from the Sheffield evaluation studies (project paper 40).

Ward L (1982) People first – developing services in the community for people with mental handicap (project paper 32).

Ward L (1984) Planning for people: developing a local service for people with mental handicap. 1. Recruiting and training staff (project paper 47).

Sang B and O'Brien J (1984) Advocacy: the UK and American experiences (project paper 51).

Oswin M (1984) They keep going away: a critical study of short-term residential care services for children who are mentally handicapped.

Porterfield J and Gathercole C (1985) The employment of people with mental handicap: progress towards an ordinary working life (project paper 55).

Richardson A and Ritchie J (1986) Making the break: parents' views about adults with a mental handicap leaving the parental home.

Ward L (ed) (1987) Getting better all the time? Issues and strategies for ensuring quality in community services for people with mental handicap (project paper 66).

Davies L (1987) Quality, costs and 'an ordinary life': comparing the costs and quality of different residential services for people with mental handicap (project paper 67).

Ann Shearer's *Building Community* and *They Keep Going Away* by Maureen Oswin are available through bookshops or from Oxford University Press Bookshop, Freepost, 116 High Street, Oxford OX1 4BR. All other titles are available from Book Sales, King's Fund Centre, 126 Albert Street, London NW1 7NF.

Further reading

PART ONE: REVALUING PEOPLE WITH LEARNING DISABILITIES

Chapter 1   Exploring values as the basis for service development

O'Brien J and Tyne A (1981) The principle of normalisation: a foundation for effective services. London, Campaign for People with Mental Handicaps. A straightforward account of normalisation with exercises designed to increase understanding of basic ideas and their practical implications.

O'Brien J (1987) A guide to personal futures planning. In: Bellamy G T and Willcox B (eds). A comprehensive guide to the activities catalog: an alternative curriculum for youth and adults with severe disabilities. Baltimore, Paul H Brookes. A statement of service objectives in terms of five key accomplishments for people with learning disabilities.

Wolfensberger W (ed) (1972) The principle of normalization in human services. Toronto, National Institute on Mental Retardation. Still the most comprehensive standard text on normalization as developed in North America.

Flynn R and Nitsch K (eds) (1980) Normalization, social integration and community services. Baltimore, University Park Press. Papers on the theory and practice of normalisation after a decade of application in North America.

Chapter 2   Involving people with learning disabilities

Carle N (1984) Key concepts in community-based services. London, Campaign for People with Mental Handicaps. A quick, but meaty, introduction to ten central issues.

Harper G and Dobson J (1985) Participation: report of a workshop involving people with mental handicaps and staff who work with them. London, Campaign for People with Mental Handicaps. A valuable source of ideas for putting on local events.

Williams P and Shoultz B (1982) We can speak for ourselves. London, Souvenir Press. Describes self-advocacy in America and Britain, with practical information for groups and advisers.

PART TWO: DESIGNING, DEVELOPING AND SAFEGUARDING
HIGH QUALITY SERVICES

General

Independent Development Council for People with Mental
Handicap (1983) Elements of a comprehensive local service for
people with mental handicap. London, IDC. A succinct guide to
services required through the life cycle to support people with
learning disabilities and their families in the community.

Shearer A (1986) Building community with people with mental
handicaps, their families and friends. London, Campaign for
People with Mental Handicaps and King Edward's Hospital Fund
for London. Excellent descriptions of the full range of local
services developed on 'an ordinary life' principles.

Craft M, Bicknell J and Hollins S (eds) (1985) Mental handicap: a
multidisciplinary approach. London, Ballière Tindall. Useful
accounts of the different professional contributions to establishing effective individual programmes for people with learning
disabilities. Also provides an overview of services for families and
children and more detailed discussion of education.

Chapter 3   A community approach to serving children and their families

Russell P and Griffiths M (1985) Working together with handicapped children. London, Souvenir Press. Explores the principles
underpinning comprehensive multi-professional services for
children with disabilities and the involvement of parents.

Mittler P and McConachie H (eds) (1983) Parents, professionals
and mentally handicapped people: approaches to partnership.
London, Croom Helm. Explores practical and conceptual issues
in partnership between parents and professionals including the
transition to adult life.

Oswin M (1984) They keep going away. London, King Edward's
Hospital Fund for London. A critical review of respite care
schemes for children with learning disabilities providing guidelines for planning sensitive local services.

Vaughan M and Shearer A (1985) Mainstreaming in Massachusetts.
London, Centre for Studies on Integration in Education and
Campaign for People with Mental Handicaps. The experience of
integration in education.

162

Chapter 4   An ordinary home life

King's Fund (1982) An ordinary life: comprehensive locally-based residential services for mentally handicapped people (project paper 24). London, King Edward's Hospital Fund for London. The original statement of principles and planning guidance for developing residential services using ordinary housing.

Mansell J, Felce D, Jenkins J, de Kock U and Toogood S (1987) Developing staffed housing for people with mental handicaps. Tunbridge Wells, Costello. A comprehensive guide to issues in planning and implementing residential services.

Camden Society for Mentally Handicapped People (1982) A decade for change. London, CSMH. An innovative voluntary agency strategy for promoting community-based services.

Heginbotham C (1984) Webs and mazes. London, Centre on Environment for the Handicapped. A guide to ways round the bureaucratic and financial obstacles involved in developing housing projects.

Chapter 5   Developing opportunities for an ordinary community life

King's Fund (forthcoming) An ordinary community life. London, King Edward's Hospital Fund for London. A systematic examination of what is involved in promoting opportunities for participation in the community by people with learning disabilities.

Atkinson D and Ward L (1986) A part of the community: social integration and neighbourhood networks. London, Campaign for People with Mental Handicaps. Provides examples of various forms of community participation.

Open University/MENCAP (1986) Mental handicap: patterns for living. Milton Keynes, Open University Press. An educational pack for families, staff and volunteers involved in the lives of people with learning disabilities, with practical suggestions on how to relate the contents to the reader's own life.

Walsh J (1986) Let's make friends. London, Souvenir Press. Linking up people with learning disabilities with other people in a 'friendship scheme'.

Lord J (1981) Participation: expanding community and leisure experiences for people with severe handicaps. Toronto, National Institute on Mental Retardation. Practical steps to enable people with severe learning disabilities to become active participants in the life and activities of their local communities.

Chapter 6   Promoting opportunities for employment

King's Fund (1984) An ordinary working life: vocational services for people with mental handicap (project paper 50). London, King Edward's Hospital Fund for London. The original statement on the importance of work in people's lives with proposals for the components of a vocational service for people with learning disabilities.

Porterfield J and Gathercole C (1985) The employment of people with mental handicap: progress towards an ordinary working life (project paper 55). London, King Edward's Hospital Fund for London. Complements *An Ordinary Working Life* with details of current employment initiatives and their benefits for people with learning disabilities.

Independent Development Council for People with Mental Handicap (1985) Living like other people. London, IDC. Discusses the full range of service provision outside the home and suggests a strategy for improving the opportunities available to people with learning disabilities for participation with non-handicapped people.

Chapter 8   Serving people with very challenging behaviour

Blunden R and Allen D (eds) (1987) Facing the challenge: an ordinary life for people with learning difficulties and challenging behaviour (project page 74). London, King Edward's Hospital Fund for London. A systematic statement of principles and design guidance for serving people with challenging behaviour within community-based local services.

Casey K, McGee J, Stark J and Menolascino F (1985) A community-based system for the mentally retarded: the ENCOR experience. Lincoln, Nebraska, University of Nebraska Press. An overview of the ENCOR service including a particularly helpful account of their techniques and approach to people with challenging behaviour.

Lovett H (1985) Cognitive counselling and persons with special needs. New York, Praeger. An unusual and stimulating book packed with examples from the author's experience of working with people with special needs.

Chapter 9   Safeguarding quality

Independent Development Council for People with Mental Handicap (1986) Pursuing quality: How good are your local services for people with mental handicap? London, IDC. This booklet sets out a practical 'quality action' approach to pursuing quality within services for people with learning difficulties.

Peters T J and Waterman R H (1982) In search of excellence: lessons from America's best-run companies. New York, Harper & Row. Examines the characteristics of commercial organisations which have a reputation for excellence.

PART THREE – ACHIEVING LARGE-SCALE CHANGE

General

Welsh Office (1982) Report of the all-Wales working party on services for mentally handicapped people. Cardiff, Welsh Office. A clear statement of a national strategy based upon the principles of *An ordinary life*.

House of Commons (1985) Community care with special reference to adult mentally ill and mentally handicapped people. Second report from the Social Services Committee, session 1984–5, Volume I. London, HMSO. An authoritative argument for comprehensive community-based services for people with learning disabilities and powerful critique of current weaknesses in policy and implementation.

Audit Commission (1986) Making a reality of community care. London, HMSO. Further strong criticism of irrationalities in current national policies and financial arrangements.

Bristol and Weston Health Authority (1986) Mental handicap services: a plan for implementation. Bristol, Bristol and Weston DHA. A detailed specification of service design, staffing and financial issues involved in implementing comprehensive local services.

Chapter 10   Generating policy and action

North Western Regional Health Authority (1983) Services for people with mental handicap: a model district service. Manchester, NWRHA. Regional guidance to local agencies on service design.

North Western Regional Health Authority (1984) Mental handicap funding policy. Manchester, NWRHA. Financial policies to support the substantive strategy.

North Western Regional Health Authority (1987) Implementing and staffing a model district service. Manchester, NWRHA. Further guidance on key implementation issues.

Chapter 11   Training for service development

Korman N and Glennerster H (1985) Closing a hospital: the Darenth Park project. London, Bedford Square Press. Detailed account of one RHA's approach to change with useful lessons for more appropriate strategies.

Quinn J B (1980) Strategies for change: logical incrementalism. Homewood, Illinois, Irvin. Provides an extensive discussion of incrementalist approaches to change in organisations.

National Health Service Training Authority (1986) Services for people with mental handicap: human resource issues. Bristol, NHSTA. A pooling of local experience on key issues in staffing, training and implementation.

Chapter 12   Managing strategic change

South Western Regional Health Authority (1986) Achieving high-quality community-based services for people with learning disabilities in the South West. Bristol, SWRHA. A sensitive account of the full range of implementation issues being addressed through the South Western strategy.

Parston G (ed) (1986) Managers as strategists: health service managers reflecting on practice. London, King Edward's Hospital Fund for London. General insights from research and practice in the field of strategic management.

Peters T and Austin N (1985) A passion for excellence: the leadership difference. London, Collins. A follow-up to *In Search of Excellence* which examines what leaders need to do in practice to build successful organisations.

IDC publications are available from the Independent Development Council for People with Mental Handicap, 126 Albert Street, London NW1 7NF. CMH publications are available from

Campaign for People with Mental Handicaps, Publications Office, 5 Kentings, Comberton, Cambs CB3 7DT. CMH also stocks some North American publications on normalisation (including the work of O'Brien and Wolfensberger). Publications cited here can be consulted at the King's Fund Centre Library, 126 Albert Street, London NW1 7NF (01–267 6111).